3STORY

Conversations
WITH JESUS

GETTING IN ON GOD'S STORY | A 3STORY DEVO

[YOUTH FOR CHRIST]

ZONDERVAN®

GRAND RAPIDS, MICHIGAN 49530 USA

ZONDERVAN.COM/
AUTHOR**TRACKER**

www.invertbooks.com

Conversations with Jesus: Getting in on God's Story
Copyright ©2006 by Youth for Christ

Youth Specialties products, 300 South Pierce Street, El Cajon, CA 92020 are published by Zondervan, 5300 Patterson Avenue Southeast, Grand Rapids, MI 49530.

Library of Congress Cataloging-in-Publication Data

Conversations with Jesus : connecting my story with God's story / by Youth for Christ.
    p. cm.
"A 3story devotional."
Includes index.
ISBN-10: 0-310-27346-3
ISBN-13: 978-0-310-27346-2
1. Youth—Prayer-books and devotions—English. I. Youth for Christ/USA.
BV4531.3.C66 2006
242'.63—dc22

2006014796

Creative Team: Dave Urbanski, Kristi Robison, Heather Haggerty, Janie Wilkerson, and Mark Novelli, IMAGO MEDIA
Cover design by Gearbox
Printed in the United States

07 08 09 10 • 8 7 6 5

TABLE OF CONTENTS

INTRODUCTION

Welcome to Our Story,from One of the "Group of Listeners"

This little book is not an ordinary book. We believe God speaks clearly through his Word and through his Spirit. Are you listening? Join us on a great adventure. The living Christ speaks today. He still guides the humble. No detail of our stories escapes his concern. He is lovingly attentive to his creation, even you and me!

Last fall we decided to listen better to the One who speaks quiet words of love. We wondered if it was okay to put those words in writing for others to read. We weren't sure if we'd be offending God by making it look like we thought we could speak for him. (Who can actually speak for God? Only God, right?) After lots of prayer and listening to the Holy Spirit, we decided to take the risk.

My friend Kate listens to Jesus much more carefully than anyone I know. She's teaching me to listen better. She's humble in her listening. Kate thinks we can all hear from God's Spirit on a regular basis. I'm starting to believe her. I'm hearing his voice more. Our group of listeners is hearing his voice more, too.

Since I'm still a beginner in the *listening process*, the idea of messages that might come from Jesus seems wild, heroic, even scary. When you consider that God Almighty might really want to say something important to you right now, today—WOW! That is freaky! And thrilling.

Our group of listeners decided to take the plunge into God's Word and urgently seek him by listening and waiting before we put anything to pen and paper. It's not been easy. Some of us struggled with spiritual battles and attacks on our souls and in the lives of our families. We felt the weight of listening to God on behalf of others like you. We hope God will be honored by the work of our ears, our hearts, and our words.

Certainly we aren't in any advanced state of spiritual growth, but we have made progress toward Jesus individually and together. The idea we pursued was abiding in Jesus and in his love. We wanted to connect our stories more intimately with God's story. That's abiding. Listening to God is one powerful way of abiding in Christ. Check out what Jesus says in John 15 about abiding:

> Abide in me, and I in you. As the branch cannot bear fruit by itself, unless it abides in the vine, neither can you, unless you abide in me. I am the vine; you are the branches. Whoever abides in me and I in him, he it is that bears much fruit, for apart from me you can do nothing. If you abide in me, and my words abide in you, ask whatever you wish, and it will be done for you. As the Father has loved me, so have I loved you. Abide in my love. If you keep my commandments, you will abide in my love, just as I have kept my Father's commandments and abide in his love. (4-5, 7, 9-10, ESV)

The tender understanding and compassion of Jesus Christ is filling our hearts in new ways; his loving conviction is correcting us every day; his joy and his sorrow are enabling us to receive his love. He is causing his love to overflow from him to us and then into a broken world where our friends and family members need him as much as we do.

We thank you for seeking Jesus Christ with us. We are in God's good hands together.

Our group of listeners was Tara Posen, Mike Klassen, Jack Crabtree, Dan Wolgemuth, Don Talley, Jennifer Morgan, Julie Conner, and Greg Boyer. The listeners relied on God's holy written Word for the content of the messages and the guidance of the Holy Spirit to hear his voice clearly.

Youth editors: Jay Alsdorf, Lauren Conner, Trevor Conner, Emily Donder, Brandon Harrigan, Julie Krogh, Gina Krogh, Alex Krohn, Brittany Poyer, Corinn Rotter, and Daniel Schlereth.

DEVOTIONAL 1

You Are Never Alone

TOPIC: Feeling alone

MAIN SCRIPTURE: "As I was with Moses, so I will be with you; I will never leave you nor forsake you." (Joshua 1:5)

OTHER SCRIPTURES: Deuteronomy 31:6-8; Psalm 23:4; Mark 15:33-39; John 14:16-19; John 16:4b-15; Colossians 1:27

WHAT JESUS MIGHT SAY TO YOU:
I understand your feelings of loneliness; your cries in the night when you feel like no one understands and no one cares have not gone unheard...and I do care.

I've known loneliness. While hanging on the cross, I felt the pain of abandonment. With my final breath, I cried out, "My God, my God, why have you forsaken me?" Although he dearly loved me, my Father in heaven couldn't comfort me in my darkest hour because I was carrying the sins of the world—your sin—on my shoulders, and he couldn't look at the sin. No one before me and no one after me has experienced abandonment and loneliness as deep and painful as that. I understand.

I carried your sin and faced the abandonment of my Father so I could free you from loneliness. Even if you can't see me now, I'm always with you because I live in you. I will never, never leave you nor forsake you. When others fail you or abandon you, I am with you—always.

In moments of desperation allow your loneliness to drive you closer to me. Don't fill your emptiness with things that can't satisfy. Lean into me—I'm as close as the air you breathe. Cry out to me in pain and remember that I cry out in pain with you.

You mean more than the world to me, so take this opportunity to remove yourself from the cares of this world and draw closer to the one who will always be with you.

Your faithful Friend, Jesus

SUMMARY CHALLENGE: Allow your loneliness to drive you closer to Jesus.

JOURNALING OPPORTUNITY:

DEVOTIONAL 2

Leaving the Past Where It Belongs

TOPIC: The difference between guilt and conviction

MAIN SCRIPTURES: "So now there is no condemnation for those who belong to Christ Jesus. For the power of the life-giving Spirit has freed you through Christ Jesus from the power of sin that leads to death. The law of Moses could not save us, because of our sinful nature. But God put into effect a different plan to save us. He sent his own Son in a human body like ours, except that ours are sinful. God destroyed sin's control over us by giving his Son as a sacrifice for our sins. He did this so that the requirement of the law would be fully accomplished for us who no longer follow our sinful nature but instead follow the Spirit." (Romans 8:1-4, NLT)

"Yet now I am happy, not because you were made sorry, but because your sorrow led you to repentance...Godly sorrow brings repentance that leads to salvation and leaves no regret, but worldly sorrow brings death." (2 Corinthians 7:9-10)

OTHER SCRIPTURES: Psalm 103:12; Acts 13:38-39; Romans 4:7-8; Romans 5:16-19; Romans 8:33-39; Ephesians 5:26-27; Jude 24

WHAT JESUS MIGHT SAY TO YOU:
Do you ever feel guilty for something you've done? Does it still haunt you? Do you wish you could go back and change it?

Sin is destructive. It damages your heart, your memories, and your relationships. It blocks your connection with me. Sin put me on the cross. I died to destroy it...to destroy its hold on your life.

Because you believe in me, you are no longer a slave to sin. You are 100 percent innocent in my eyes, fully forgiven...past, present, and future. Your slate is clean. Your sins are as far from you as East is from West. I will never hold anything against you.

Why then do you still live with guilt? It's because you have not forgiven yourself. Yes, sin has consequences you must work through...but guilt? It's unnecessary and only keeps you a slave to sin. Because of me, you are freed from guilt. No regrets. No condemnation. However, someone does oppose your freedom.

Satan doesn't want you to experience forgiveness. By beating you over the head with past sins, he can distract you...deter you from living the amazing, effective life I desire for you.

Sinning means turning from me and choosing your own way. When you do, your heart will ache because my Spirit lives in you. This is called conviction. Do not confuse it with guilt. When you sin, my heart breaks—that affects our relationship. Your response, then, should be to confess and restore your relationship with me, turn from your sin, understand you are forgiven, forgive yourself, and move on...in freedom...without guilt.

Don't listen to the voice of guilt. Ignore Satan. Remember my love for you. Forgive yourself as I've forgiven you. Be free.

For your freedom, Jesus

SUMMARY CHALLENGE: Don't be a slave to guilt; your freedom was purchased at a high price.

JOURNALING OPPORTUNITY:

DEVOTIONAL 3

Note to Self

TOPIC: Knowing who you really are

MAIN SCRIPTURE: "Yet I could have confidence in myself if anyone could. If others have reason for confidence in their own efforts, I have even more! For I was circumcised when I was eight days old, having been born into a pure-blooded Jewish family that is a branch of the tribe of Benjamin. So I am a real Jew if there ever was one! What's more, I was a member of the Pharisees, who demand the strictest obedience to the Jewish law. And zealous? Yes, in fact, I harshly persecuted the church. And I obeyed the Jewish law so carefully that I was never accused of any fault. I once thought all these things were so very important, but now I consider them worthless because of what Christ has done. Yes, everything else is worthless when compared with the priceless gain of knowing Christ Jesus my Lord. I have discarded everything else, counting it all as garbage, so that I may have Christ and become one with him. I no longer count on my own goodness or my ability to obey God's law, but I trust Christ to save me. For God's way of making us right with himself depends on faith." (Philippians 3:4-9, NLT)

OTHER SCRIPTURES: Galatians 2:20; Galatians 6:14; 1 John 5:20

WHAT JESUS MIGHT SAY TO YOU:
Take note...at your deepest place, at the core of who you are: *You are not a son or a daughter. You are not a sister or a brother. You are not a student or a dropout. You are not smart or not-so-smart. You are not needed or unnecessary. You are not cool or uncool. You are not an original or a slave to fashion. You are not funny or lame. You are not an artist or uncreative. You are not*

outgoing or shy. You are not popular or a loner. You are not a role model or a rebel.

These are the masks you may try to hide behind, the places you may run to for shelter, the idols you may bow before. But your identity can't be found in any of these things. You can't become more valuable by building up any of these things. You can't become less valuable by lacking any of these things. You can't be completely fulfilled by relying on or investing in these things.

At your deepest place, at the core of who you are: *You are loved by me. You are simply a naked spirit clothed by my grace. You are my child. You are completely known. You are forgiven. You are brand new. You are precious in my sight. You are held close. You are treasured, and I will never let you go. You are secure, and I will never let you down. You have been chosen to be my friend and coworker. Your heart is my home. You are my beloved. I want you, not the things you hide behind.*

Remember who you really are. Let me be your source of joy, the foundation of your identity, your life.

Your Anchor, Jesus

SUMMARY CHALLENGE: Remember who you really are.

JOURNALING OPPORTUNITY:

DEVOTIONAL 4

Happiness Is Overrated

TOPIC: Jesus wants to make you whole.

MAIN SCRIPTURES: "Being confident of this, that he who began a good work in you will carry it on to completion until the day of Christ Jesus." (Philippians 1:6)

"The young man said to Him, 'All these things I have kept; what am I still lacking?' Jesus said to him, 'If you wish to be complete, go and sell your possessions and give to the poor, and you will have treasure in heaven; and come, follow Me.'" (Matthew 19:20-21, NASB)

OTHER SCRIPTURES: John 10:10; Philippians 3:8-10; Hebrews 2:10; James 1:4

WHAT JESUS MIGHT SAY TO YOU:
How will your life change as a result of knowing me?

Think about the world you live in. It's full of self-consumed people, driven by success and what they think will benefit them. It makes me sad to see how this thinking has corrupted my message of my love. People even try to say that following me will guarantee a happy, easy, problem-free life.

My child, this is not what I have in mind for you. My plan is much bigger. My desires for you are far deeper!

In my letters to you (the Bible) I often use the word *teleios*. This Greek word means in English "complete, full-grown, becoming the person I created you to be." This is my desire for you...wholeness. I want to heal your heart and enable you to experience the full life I have promised.

Warning: The road to wholeness isn't easy. It's a process. Wholeness doesn't mean problems disappear; it means that because you know me, you lack nothing and are able to weather all of life's storms. In the hard and confusing times remember this: I love you. My heart is unfailing. I'm holding you tight.

Don't ever settle for less than my absolute best for you. The world will try to convince you to take the safe, easy route. Don't cave. I love you far more than you could ever imagine, and I'm preparing you for great things. Trust my love for you. Trust me. I'm worth it.

Holding your heart, Jesus

SUMMARY CHALLENGE: Your wholeness is more important than your happiness.

JOURNALING OPPORTUNITY:

DEVOTIONAL 5

Abide Is an Action Word

TOPIC: Abiding is active.

MAIN SCRIPTURE: "Abide in Me, and I in you. As the branch cannot bear fruit of itself unless it abides in the vine, so neither can you unless you abide in Me. I am the vine, you are the branches; he who abides in Me and I in him, he bears much fruit, for apart from Me you can do nothing." (John 15:4-5, NASB)

OTHER SCRIPTURES: John 15:1-11; Galatians 2:20; James 2:17; 1 John 2:24-28; 1 John 3:18

WHAT JESUS MIGHT SAY TO YOU:

When you hear the word *abide*, what comes to mind? Do you think of someone sitting quietly in her room, locked away from the world? If so, you're missing it. Quiet time is part of abiding, but abiding is so much more! Abiding is active, a verb. It's about living with me. Abiding is the foundation of the two greatest commandments—to love me and to love others. Love is definitely an action.

Listen to all the active words that describe abiding:

Resting in me.

Becoming more like me.

Surrendering everything to me.

Learning to listen and hear my voice.

Depending on me in all things...good or bad.

Making your home in me as I make my home in your heart.

Being real with me: inviting me into your pain and your struggles.

Hanging out with me: inviting me to join you in every aspect of your life.

Getting to know me through my Story (the Bible), talking with me, and asking questions.

Listening to others so that you can know them better and see their needs.

Serving others to show them that I am able to meet their needs.

Loving others with the love I've shown you.

Building into the lives of others.

Encouraging others.

Abiding is absolutely necessary. Your one job is to stay connected to me. I am the Vine; I will produce the fruit. But staying connected to me requires effort.

I have plans for you to do great things...but apart from me you can do nothing. Make me your supply. Let my love flow through you to others. Let it move you to action. This is abiding.

Your Vine, Jesus

SUMMARY CHALLENGE: Abiding in Jesus doesn't automatically happen—you have to take the first step.

JOURNALING OPPORTUNITY:

DEVOTIONAL 6

Experiencing God's Peace in the Middle of Worry

TOPIC: Worrying about things

MAIN SCRIPTURE: "Don't worry about anything; instead, pray about everything. Tell God what you need, and thank him for all he has done. If you do this, you will experience God's peace, which is far more wonderful than the human mind can understand. His peace will guard your hearts and minds as you live in Christ Jesus." (Philippians 4:6-7, NLT)

OTHER SCRIPTURES: Exodus 16:16-21; Matthew 6:25-34; Mark 4:34-41

WHAT JESUS MIGHT SAY TO YOU:

Why do you worry and get upset? Have you forgotten how wide and long and high and deep my love is for you? I love you more than life itself. If I can calm the stormiest sea, heal the sick, and raise the dead...if I can overcome death and the grave...then know that my great power far surpasses your greatest problem.

At this very moment the Holy Spirit and I are praying for you to your Father in heaven. We're for you; we're on your side. But best of all your Father in heaven is for you, too. And if God is for you, who can stand against you?

We are praying that you will accept the peace we offer you—peace that's far more wonderful than you can understand, peace that guards your heart and mind as you walk with me. But you need to let go of your worry before you can hold on to my peace.

You don't need to be anxious about tomorrow because tomorrow will care for itself. Worrying will do nothing to change it. Worrying only fools you into believing that you can change your situation and save yourself. But you can't. I'm the only one who can save you. Don't load yourself up with burdens that don't belong to you. My yoke is easy and my burden is light.

When you struggle with worry, tell me exactly how you feel. Remember how I have taken care of you in the past. Trust that I am in control of your future regardless of what happens right now. Rather than focusing on your problems, focus on me, trusting that I want to solve your problems.

Your true peace, Jesus

SUMMARY CHALLENGE: Rather than focusing on your problems, focus on the problem solver.

JOURNALING OPPORTUNITY:

DEVOTIONAL 7

Risk the Relationship

TOPIC: Experiencing broken trust

MAIN SCRIPTURE: "The LORD is my strength and my shield; my heart trusts in him, and I am helped. My heart leaps for joy and I will give thanks to him in song." (Psalm 28:7)

OTHER SCRIPTURES: Isaiah 26:3; Matthew 11:28; Matthew 26:47-56; Romans 12:21; 2 Timothy 2:13

WHAT JESUS MIGHT SAY TO YOU:

Few things hurt as much as trusting someone only to discover that the person can't be trusted. Without trust a friendship simply does not exist.

I understand your feelings of betrayal, the humiliation of being exposed, and the regret of friendship gone sour. One of my closest followers betrayed me, and it ended up getting me nailed to a cross.

The fact is, no one is completely trustworthy—except me. Others will always let you down, and you will let others down, too. In fact, you've let me down at times (you know all about it, so we don't need to get into it), and you will continue to do so in the future. But that doesn't change my undying love for you.

The question is: Where do you go from here?

You can strike back at the person who hurt you, or you can respond in the same way that I always respond to you—with forgiveness and love. Rather than allowing evil to overcome you, overcome evil with good.

You can stay angry, or you can give me your anger. It's okay

CONVERSATIONS WITH JESUS

to tell the person who broke your trust how you feel, but if you take out your anger on that person, you'll probably do or say something you'll later regret. You're better off venting your frustrations on me because I can handle it.

Most important, you can promise yourself that you'll never trust anyone again, or you can risk entering into other trusting relationships. Taking the risk of trusting and being betrayed can be painful, but the alternative—avoiding true relationships altogether—is far worse.

Your trustworthy Friend, Jesus

SUMMARY CHALLENGE: Take the risk of trusting and being betrayed; don't avoid true relationships.

JOURNALING OPPORTUNITY:

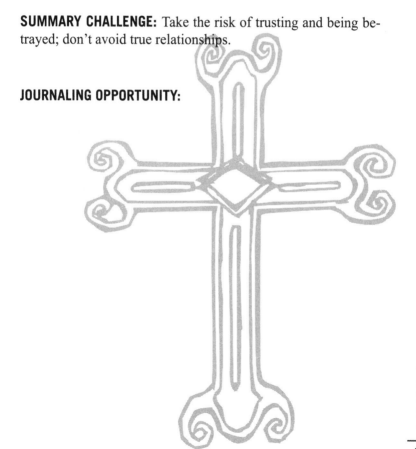

DEVOTIONAL 8

Contentment Only Comes from Christ

TOPIC: Materialism

MAIN SCRIPTURE: "I am not saying this because I am in need, for I have learned to be content whatever the circumstances. I know what it is to be in need, and I know what it is to have plenty. I have learned the secret of being content in any and every situation, whether well fed or hungry, whether living in plenty or in want. I can do everything through him who gives me strength." (Philippians 4:11-13)

OTHER SCRIPTURES: Deuteronomy 4:24; Deuteronomy 6:1-8; 1 Kings 3:5-14; Proverbs 11:28; Ecclesiastes 5:10-12; Jeremiah 9:23-24; Matthew 6:19-33; Romans 1:24-25; 2 Corinthians 8:9; 1 Timothy 6:6-10; 1 John 2:15-16

WHAT JESUS MIGHT SAY TO YOU:
What is your heart's greatest desire? Is it me...or something else?

Every time you assume your next purchase will make you happier...every time you dream about winning the lottery and suppose that it will solve all your problems...every time you look in the mirror and allow it to tell you how much you're worth... my heart aches.

It aches because I know you're setting yourself up for disappointment. But even more it aches because I want to be your greatest desire above anyone or anything else! I want you to understand that I am enough for you.

Riches and the things of this world are not evil in and of themselves. You can enjoy them and love me at the same time. But when you allow them to compete with me to become your greatest desires, they're no different from the idols my people worshiped in the Bible.

I'm jealous for your love. And can you blame me? I surrendered the riches of heaven to purchase your salvation with my blood. I have held nothing back from you. When you have me, you have everything!

Don't look to money or stuff for contentment because they never really satisfy. They only leave you craving more. You were wired to experience the contentment that only comes from me.

Filling your heart, Jesus

SUMMARY CHALLENGE: Seek Jesus and you will find him. He'll make sure you have everything you need—including contentment.

JOURNALING OPPORTUNITY:

DEVOTIONAL 9

No Fear of Failure

TOPIC: Lacking self-confidence

MAIN SCRIPTURE: "Be bold and strong! Banish fear and doubt! For remember, the Lord your God is with you wherever you go." (Joshua 1:9, Living Bible)

OTHER SCRIPTURES: Matthew 25:14-30; 1 Corinthians 15:57; Philippians 1:6

WHAT JESUS MIGHT SAY TO YOU:
Don't live in fear today. Don't withdraw from the world and all the opportunities I give you.

Don't be afraid to fail. Be confident today. Jump into new and challenging situations. You have nothing to worry about. I'm not like some coach pulling you off the field or cutting you from the team if you strike out or drop the ball. You belong to me. What I started doing in your life I promise to finish. You will see the finished results when we finally see each other face to face.

Every day I put you in situations where you can grow and become stronger. Some are rough and scary, but when you ask me to help—I'll be there. Don't give up. You can do all things through me and the strength I give you.

Don't shy away from taking chances. Remember the story I told about the boss who gave money to three men so they could invest it? The only one who disappointed the boss was the guy who buried the money in a safe place rather than taking a chance and investing it. I'm the master in that story and in your life.

Take some risks and use the talents, abilities, and opportunities I've given you. Don't bury them. Depend on me and watch them all grow.

Your reason for confidence, Jesus

SUMMARY CHALLENGE: Following Jesus isn't about perfection. Live boldly. Take risks for God. God will teach you to trust him through your successes and failures.

JOURNALING OPPORTUNITY:

DEVOTIONAL 10

Picking Up the Pieces of a Broken Heart

TOPIC: Broken hearts

MAIN SCRIPTURE: "Whom have I in heaven but you? And there is nothing on earth that I desire besides you. My flesh and my heart may fail, but God is the strength of my heart and my portion forever." (Psalm 73:25-26, ESV)

OTHER SCRIPTURES: Romans 8:8-30; 1 Corinthians 13:4-8; Revelation 21:4

WHAT JESUS MIGHT SAY TO YOU:

How do you pick up the shattered pieces of a broken heart? You can't—but I can. My heart aches with you. Your hurts are my hurts. Your tears are my tears. I understand and feel the depths of your pain because I have suffered disappointment, betrayal, rejection, and abandonment, too. I feel your pain, but I am also present in your pain and can work all things for your good because I love you.

The easy way through this is to numb your aching heart. To say, "I'll never let anyone hurt me again." To become angry, bitter, and vengeful. But do you really think that by hiding your heart, you can make the pain go away? It won't work. It only prolongs the pain. Love can't exist without the potential for being hurt. To risk love you must also risk pain. If you have to choose between risking a broken heart and knowing you'll feel nothing, you are always better off risking a broken heart. What kind of life can you enjoy when you feel nothing?

I am the strength of your heart and everything you need—forever. No one can fill the hole inside but me. No one can heal your wounds but me. So share your deepest aches, feelings, and frustrations with me because I can handle them. Bring the shattered pieces of your broken heart to me and let me put it back together again. But I promise you, what I put together will look different from what existed before. You'll discover that what I make looks a lot like me.

The Healer of your heart, Jesus

SUMMARY CHALLENGE: Bring Jesus the shattered pieces of your broken heart and let him put it back together again. (Psalm 56:3)

JOURNALING OPPORTUNITY:

DEVOTIONAL 11

Receiving Encouragement Instead of Despair

TOPIC: Needing encouragement

MAIN SCRIPTURE: "Whom have I in heaven but you? I desire you more than anything on earth. My health may fail, and my spirit may grow weak, but God remains the strength of my heart; he is mine forever." (Psalm 73:25-26, NLT)

OTHER SCRIPTURES: Psalm 42; Proverbs 13:12; Ecclesiastes 4:9-12; Lamentations 3; Jeremiah 29:11-14; Philippians 2:1-4

WHAT JESUS MIGHT SAY TO YOU:

We all face different seasons in our lives: Spring, when everything comes to life, and new birth, fresh ideas, and fruitfulness abound...summer, when everyone is at play, friendships flourish, and hope is fulfilled...fall, when people are hard at work but also enjoy the fruits of their labors...and winter, when everything seems cold and dead, so rather than venture outdoors, people live by themselves in despair and isolation.

I know that your feelings of discouragement and despair make life miserable for you. But remember that it's only a season. It won't last forever—spring is right around the corner. Also remember that this probably isn't the last winter you will face. More will come, as will more seasons of spring, summer, and fall.

During this cold season of your life, I know you're tempted to avoid venturing outside and feeling the frigid outdoors. It's easier to keep to yourself than to share your pain with someone else. But isolating yourself will do nothing to resolve your despair. If anything, it will only make it worse. This is a good time to seek friends who will encourage you and offer you the warmth of their friendship.

But did you also know that in the cold place where you live, I live, too? I am alive and well in every season of your life. Your despair can drive you away from me, or it can lead you toward me, where you will feel the warmth of my friendship. When you seek me with your whole heart, you will find me. I am your hope, your encouragement, and the strength of your heart.

Your encouragement, Jesus

SUMMARY CHALLENGE: During your cold seasons of despair, seek the warmth that comes from friendships—especially your friendship with Jesus.

JOURNALING OPPORTUNITY:

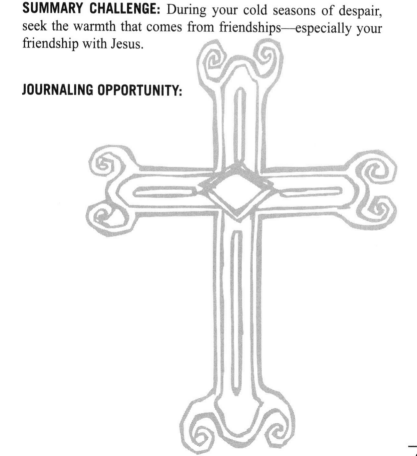

DEVOTIONAL 12

Be Who You Are

TOPIC: Fear of intimacy

MAIN SCRIPTURE: "So do not be afraid of them. There is nothing concealed that will not be disclosed, or hidden that will not be made known. What I tell you in the dark, speak in the daylight; what is whispered in your ear, proclaim from the roofs. Do not be afraid of those who kill the body but cannot kill the soul." (Matthew 10:26-28)

OTHER SCRIPTURES: Psalm 139:14-16; Luke 9:24; Philippians 3:10; 1 John 4:18

WHAT JESUS MIGHT SAY TO YOU:

I realize that entering into true relationship is risky. What if people don't like what—or who—they see? Instead of suffering the seemingly unbearable pain of rejection, the easy alternative is to build walls around your heart that no one can penetrate. By acting funny, smart, clueless, sexy, quiet, nice, tough, or whatever, you can keep people away from the real you. Unfortunately, those walls keep me away from you as well.

Don't be afraid of being who you are. I'm crazy about you. I wired you for relationships that go far beyond trivial matters and surface conversations. I created you for intimacy with others... and with me.

But you can't drink from the cup of relationships without tasting pain. The two go together. When relationships happen, pain happens right in the middle of them. But pain isn't the worst thing that can happen to you. The worst thing that can happen to you is to spend your life with a heart that feels no pain, a heart that is hardened to me and to the people around you.

Only through truly intimate relationships will you experience the satisfaction that comes from being loved for who you are, not what you do. That's how I love you.

So be who you are. Risk relationships. Tear down the walls that keep people from knowing the real you. And remember that I love you just the way you are!

Your Creator, Jesus

SUMMARY CHALLENGE: Take the risk of being who you are in your relationships, and you'll experience the satisfaction that comes from being loved for who you are, not for what you do.

JOURNALING OPPORTUNITY:

DEVOTIONAL 13

No Reason to Quit

TOPIC: Hope

MAIN SCRIPTURE: "All honor to God, the God and Father of our Lord Jesus Christ; for it is his boundless mercy that has given us the privilege of being born again, so that we are now members of God's own family. Now we live in the hope of eternal life because Christ rose again from the dead." (1 Peter 1:3, Living Bible)

OTHER SCRIPTURES: Romans 5:1-5; Romans 12:12; 2 Corinthians 1:10

WHAT JESUS MIGHT SAY TO YOU:

You and I are hooked together for life...and for all eternity. I am your hope...your best and only hope. Through me your sins are forgiven, and you have become a member of God's family forever. Through me your life has been given purpose and significance. Through me you have the strength to live through suffering and hard times.

Hope in me makes you strong. When challenges and trouble come, you can know I am with you. I'll help you get through them or turn them into positive things. Even when the worst happens, your hope can be unshaken because I am with you. I am in control of everything. Even bad events in your life can bring good results. You can come through tough times with bigger spiritual and emotional muscles, along with the confidence that you can count on me every time.

Hope in me keeps you going when you're exhausted and discouraged. Trust me and live for me. I will show you the extravagant dimensions of my grace. You will be rewarded for faithfully following me. You and I will live together in my kingdom forever. It will all be worth it.

Never give up on yourself because I have not given up on you.

Your friends need my hope. Without it life is grim. Listen to their cries for help. Show them the hope you have in me. Never give up on anyone. Even your hardest-to-reach friends can find me. You can help.

Your reason for living, Jesus

SUMMARY CHALLENGE: How can people go through hurricanes, disasters, and personal losses and still focus on a better future? It's with hope—God's hope!

JOURNALING OPPORTUNITY:

DEVOTIONAL 14

Why Is God Smiling?

TOPIC: God is proud of you

MAIN SCRIPTURE: "Moreover because of what Christ has done, we have become gifts to God that he delights in, for as part of God's sovereign plan we were chosen from the beginning to be his, and all things happen just as he decided long ago. God's purpose in this was that we should praise God and give glory to him for doing these mighty things for us, who were the first to trust in Christ." (Ephesians 1:11-12, Living Bible)

OTHER SCRIPTURES: 2 Corinthians 2:14; Ephesians 2:4-6

WHAT JESUS MIGHT SAY TO YOU:
Saying your name makes me smile. Listening to your prayers grips my heart. I love you so much. I'm proud of you. I talk to the Father about you. I keep track of the smallest details of your life. The skeptics say that's impossible. (Their small ideas about me make us all laugh in heaven.) Don't worry. I can handle the weight of the world and much more. No problem.

I have made a place for you here in heaven, a place you can't begin to imagine or comprehend. No words in any language adequately explain it. You will be here with me forever. I am well connected—and now through me, you are, too.

I love it when you make others aware of the reason for your joy and hope. I love to hear you tell your friends that I am your friend. You're worth the exorbitant price I had to pay for your ransom.

Looking forward to all of eternity with you, Jesus

SUMMARY CHALLENGE: "No eye has seen, no ear has heard, no mind has conceived what God has prepared for those who love him." (1 Corinthians 2:9)

JOURNALING OPPORTUNITY:

DEVOTIONAL 15

Someone in Heaven Loves You

TOPIC: Lack of a father's love

MAIN SCRIPTURE: "Father to the fatherless, defender of widows—this is God, whose dwelling is holy." (Psalm 68:5, NLT)

OTHER SCRIPTURES: Psalm 27:10; Psalm 34:17-18; Psalm 147:3

WHAT JESUS MIGHT SAY TO YOU:

Count how many of your friends live with sadness and anger. So many of them come from broken homes without loving fathers.

You've had some tough father moments, too. I know it hurts when a father gives no words of love to his children.

Do you see the hurts your friends absorb every week? Their pain grows until it becomes numbness. They need my love. Can you let them know that their heavenly Father loves them?

That's a tough assignment. When an earthly father lets you down, it's easy to get bitter and push everyone away—especially the heavenly Father. When your friends seem hard and angry toward me, show them that my love is real. Listen to their stories. It will probably take awhile to get them out. Be patient. Treat them the way I treated hurting people. They need comfort and encouragement. That's love in action. They may not have anyone else to turn to. When the time is right, let them know that your listening ear and your unconditional love come from your heavenly Father. My heart breaks for them. Tell them my story—I showed up on earth to prove my Father's love. Everywhere I went I told stories about fathers and children so that they (and you) can understand God's unconditional love and forgiveness.

When earthly fathers fail badly, God draws near. He is a Father to the fatherless (as well as to fathers who fail). He provides a new family to those who are lonely and brokenhearted. He hears when you call to him. Try it today. Pour out your heart to him for your friends (and your hurts, too). He cares. You'll see.

With the Father's love, Jesus

SUMMARY CHALLENGE: When earthly fathers aren't around or fail to love you, your heavenly Father keeps his promises to you. Count on it.

JOURNALING OPPORTUNITY:

DEVOTIONAL 16

You Are...

TOPIC: A righteousness not our own

MAIN SCRIPTURES: "...and be found in him, not having a righteousness of my own that comes from the law, but that which is through faith in Christ—the righteousness that comes from God and is by faith." (Philippians 3:9)

"You are the salt of the earth...You are the light of the world. A city on a hill cannot be hidden." (Matthew 5:13-14)

OTHER SCRIPTURES: Genesis 1:27; Psalm 45:11; Romans 3:21-22; Romans 10:3-4; 2 Corinthians 5:21; Hebrews 10:14

WHAT JESUS MIGHT SAY TO YOU:

Some people believe they're better than others. They think they have it together and others don't. However, I know you sometimes feel quite the opposite. You see yourself as a horrible sinner who can do nothing right and has nothing good to offer. You may even feel worthless...and then call it humility.

Contrary to popular belief, this is not humility. It's just shame and poor self-image. So what is humility? How should you see yourself?

It's true—you are a sinner. No matter how hard you try, you can never live up to my perfect standards on your own. This is why you so desperately need me. I did for you what you could never do for yourself. Through my perfect life, death, and resurrection, you've been given my righteousness and made blameless in my eyes!

In addition, you were created in my image. Everything about me is good, and therefore you also bear great good. I have given you amazing gifts. You are of infinite worth in my eyes. You enthrall me.

So when you think, "I wish I could be more..." or, "Why can't I get my act together?" I want you to remember this: You bear my image and righteousness. You just need to live like you know it's true. You are salt. You are light. You reflect me. This is who you are. Believe it. Live it!

Your glory, Jesus

SUMMARY CHALLENGE: You are perfect in Jesus' eyes; now you just need to live like you know it's true. "Humility, then, means understanding that, while you desperately need me, you also bear a great glory. A reflected glory. My glory. My goodness. You are my mirror. I earned it all, but I have chosen you to bear it, because of my great love for you." (John Eldredge, *Waking the Dead*, 77)

JOURNALING OPPORTUNITY:

DEVOTIONAL 17

No Junk

TOPIC: Dealing with a negative self-image

MAIN SCRIPTURE: "For though your hearts were once full of darkness, now you are full of light from the Lord, and your behavior should show it!" (Ephesians 5:8, NLT)

OTHER SCRIPTURES: John 10:7-15; Romans 12:1-2; 2 Corinthians 5:17; 1 Peter 2:9

WHAT JESUS MIGHT SAY TO YOU:
You're not junk. Not even close.

I'm angry when I hear the Enemy, Satan, telling you outright lies about who you are. He's the father of all liars. He's all about stealing hope, killing, and destroying people. He uses people who talk trash to you and put you down. He rejoices when the culture of celebrity brainwashes you into thinking you're not beautiful enough or cool enough. They're all lies.

Let me help you flush out all the poisonous lies you've believed about yourself. Your true value isn't defined or measured by physical beauty or your ability to achieve some big goal or entertain others. Let go of those lies. Focus on being alive and growing in me today. Find your real worth and purpose as a priceless child of God the Father. No one and nothing can ever take that away from you.

When that dark cloud of feeling dumb, ugly, or unloved hangs over your head, let me whisper the truth in your ear—you are a new creation with me in your life. The old is gone. Your past is forgiven and forgotten.

Abide with me today. Meditate on my Word and let it reprogram your mind. Listen to my voice. Believe the truth about who you are in me.

Telling you the truth, Jesus

SUMMARY CHALLENGE: Whose voice will you listen to about who you really are? Draw close and listen to what God says about you today.

JOURNALING OPPORTUNITY:

DEVOTIONAL 18

Never Enough

TOPIC: When you don't think there's enough provision (money)

MAIN SCRIPTURE: "…for I have learned how to get along happily whether I have much or little. I know how to live on almost nothing or with everything. I have learned the secret of living in every situation, whether it is with a full stomach or empty, with plenty or little. For I can do everything with the help of Christ who gives me the strength I need." (Philippians 4:11-13, NLT)

OTHER SCRIPTURES: Matthew 6:24-34; Luke 12:15-21; 1 Timothy 6:6-10

WHAT JESUS MIGHT SAY TO YOU:

How much money do you need to be happy? Most people tell me it's just a little more than they have right now. The world you live in is filled with pressure to buy, buy, buy. Advertisers try to keep you feeling dissatisfied with what you have and hungry to purchase more of the stuff they push at you. So you continue buying to keep up with what everyone else has. It's a clever trap. The more you get, the less satisfied you are with what you own.

I'm sure you want a job if you don't have one already. You want power and independence so you don't have to feel like you're begging money from your parents. But you can get so wrapped up in earning and spending money that you forget about me. Your work hours may leave you so tired that you can't find time to spend with me—to worship, read my Word, or pray anything beyond quick cries for help.

Break out of the money trap. Put me first. Find your happiness and fulfillment in relationships, not possessions.

People have always been worried about money and stuff. Don't be like the people who ignore God. They take pride in superficial things. But your heavenly Father already knows perfectly well what you need, and he will give it to you as you give him first place in your life. Don't be anxious about tomorrow. God will take care of you.

Your fulfillment, Jesus

SUMMARY CHALLENGE: "No one can serve two masters...You cannot serve both God and Money." (Matthew 6:24)

JOURNALING OPPORTUNITY:

DEVOTIONAL 19

Live Free

TOPIC: Peer pressure

MAIN SCRIPTURE: "...perfect love expels all fear. If we are afraid, it is for fear of judgment, and this shows that his love has not been perfected in us." (1 John 4:18, NLT)

OTHER SCRIPTURES: John 13:31-38; John 18:25-27; John 21:1-22

WHAT JESUS MIGHT SAY TO YOU:
Don't be afraid. I've been saying that to all of my disciples since I was here on the earth. Don't be afraid of what others think or say about you. They don't know you like I do. Don't let their opinions define who you are. My unconditional love gives you freedom to be the real you—the you I created.

That inner pressure that pushes you to do stupid, wrong, or hurtful things so other people will like you—I know that's not the real you. That junk comes from old insecurities and fears. You and I need to be connected today. I want to see the real you come alive. Be confident of my presence in your life today. My death on the cross is proof that I love you. Don't be afraid.

My disciple Peter told me peer pressure would never bother him. He bragged that he would be with me all the way even if it cost him his life. I knew better. I told him he would find out the truth about himself that same night. Did you hear what happened to him? Three times that night he denied he even knew me. The last time was to a young girl who was no threat at all to him. That broke him.

The next time I saw him, I asked him if he loved me. That's all that really mattered. It shook him up when he understood that I was never going to reject him. From that point on he started living like knowing me and obeying me was more important than his reputation with his buddies. That freed him to be the real Peter and do awesome things for me and the people around him.

That's the same connection I want with you today. Even better—when your friends see the real you living freely, with my constant love inside you, they will want to know your secret. Be ready to reveal it to them.

Live free, Jesus

SUMMARY CHALLENGE: Because peer pressure only has power when you let others' opinions become more important than God's opinions, trust God's view of you.

JOURNALING OPPORTUNITY:

DEVOTIONAL 20

What Becomes of the Brokenhearted?

TOPIC: Surviving a broken heart

MAIN SCRIPTURE: "Now the LORD observed the extent of the people's wickedness, and he saw that all their thoughts were consistently and totally evil. So the LORD was sorry he had ever made them. It broke his heart." (Genesis 6:5-6, NLT)

OTHER SCRIPTURES: Psalm 30:1-3,11-12; Psalm 34:18; Isaiah 53:3; Jeremiah 31:13

WHAT JESUS MIGHT SAY TO YOU:

Few things hurt worse than a broken heart. It feels like the end of the world. Your heart is the core of who you are. When it feels out of order, so does everything else.

Did you read my words in Genesis 6? You're not alone. My heart absolutely breaks when people turn from me and reject my love. Know that when you are hurting, I understand and am there with you. Invite me into your pain. Rest in my unchanging love for you as I carry you down the road of healing. But what does this road look like? How do we survive and move on?

In Isaiah I'm described as a man of sorrows, but I wasn't a sad man. How am I filled with joy, peace, love, and hope while suffering a broken heart? Because my Father's love sustains me.

A broken heart is not easily fixed. You may be tempted to lock up your heart and throw away the key, to protect your heart and never love again. It may seem safer, but it will only cause more pain. If you cease to love, your heart will die. Your heart was created to love because I made it. I am love. You can't truly love and experience the life I intend for you if you ignore your heart to avoid hurt. This is why I don't protect my heart from brokenness. The answer is always more love, not less. Be brokenhearted, not hard-hearted!

To live a life of love means risking a broken heart. Keep loving. Trust in me. Let me be your joy and strength. This is the way to healing. You will make it and it will be worth it.

Holding you close, Jesus

SUMMARY CHALLENGE: Don't let a broken heart be the end of love, but the beginning.

JOURNALING OPPORTUNITY:

DEVOTIONAL 21

Unlikely Heroes

TOPIC: God uses the weak and lowly

MAIN SCRIPTURES: "In the same way, was not even Rahab the prostitute considered righteous for what she did when she gave lodging to the spies and sent them off in a different direction?" (James 2:25)

"The people I treasure most are the humble—they depend only on me and tremble when I speak." (Isaiah 66:2, CEV)

OTHER SCRIPTURES: Joshua 2; Joshua 6:17; Matthew 5:1-10; 1 Corinthians 1:27

WHAT JESUS MIGHT SAY TO YOU:
Today I want to talk about your feelings of inadequacy. It's a lie that you're not good enough to follow me or represent me to the world. I know the world prizes the strong and successful. My way is different. I look for those with humble hearts, aware of their weaknesses. Those who give me room to work in them and through them. These are the people I want to use. Have you read the story of my servant Rahab in Joshua 2? Go ahead. Read it.

I chose to use Rahab in a mighty way. Why? Was it because she was popular and well-respected? No, quite the opposite. In fact, Rahab was a prostitute. But I chose her. And not only did she change the world, but she also had a profound experience of my grace and mercy in the process.

Fast-forward a few years. Rahab had a son named Boaz. Boaz is considered one of the greatest examples of grace and mercy in history. (Check out the book of Ruth.) How did Boaz learn to be so godly and merciful? It was from his mother, the former prostitute.

Remember David—the humble shepherd boy who became a great king, a king after my own heart? He was also a descendant of Rahab and Boaz. Furthermore, guess who else descended from Rahab? I did.

I would rather change the world through a humble prostitute or shepherd boy than through a prideful, religious person who thinks he has it all together. I can't use those who think they have no need for me.

Are you imperfect? Messed up? Do you need me? If the answer is yes, you're in good shape. I can use you. I want to use you to change the world...and I will.

Going against the flow, Jesus

SUMMARY CHALLENGE: No matter who you are or where you've been, God wants to use you.

JOURNALING OPPORTUNITY:

DEVOTIONAL 22

The Greatest Power

TOPIC: Love

MAIN SCRIPTURE: "So now faith, hope and love abide, these three; but the greatest of these is love." (1 Corinthians 13:13, ESV)

OTHER SCRIPTURES: John 13:34-35; 1 Thessalonians 3:12-13; 1 John 4:10-12

WHAT JESUS MIGHT SAY TO YOU:

Real love is the most powerful force in the world. To find that real love, look at what God did for you. He sent me into your selfish and evil world to give you eternal life through my death. You see real love when you see me nailed to the cross. It's not about your love for God but his love for you. He took the initiative and, driven by love, sent me to pay the price required for the forgiveness of your sins.

God's love forgives and forgets. Don't be afraid of him. Submerge yourself in his love. Tattoo it on your heart. Let love determine how you think about yourself. Let love motivate you to give and do for others like God did for you. I know you want your friends and family to believe in me. I will become real to them when they see my love in you.

Love is all about doing what is best for another person even if the cost is high for you. Love is giving...helping...building up...it's just what I do for you. You want to be like me...right? Just love people. Give and forgive.

Always loving you, Jesus

SUMMARY CHALLENGE: "And now these three remain: faith, hope and love. But the greatest of these is love." (1 Corinthians 13:13)

JOURNALING OPPORTUNITY:

DEVOTIONAL 23

God Speaks through You

TOPIC: Fear of sharing your faith

MAIN SCRIPTURE: "We are Christ's ambassadors, and God is using us to speak to you. We urge you, as though Christ himself were here pleading with you, 'Be reconciled to God!'" (2 Corinthians 5:20, NLT)

OTHER SCRIPTURES: 1 Corinthians 2:1-5; 2 Corinthians 2:16; Ephesians 6:19

WHAT JESUS MIGHT SAY TO YOU:
I know this is important for us to talk about. Sometimes this is difficult for some people who love me. They don't want to look like they're pressuring people or selling religion.

Some people want me to light up the sky and do flashy miracles, thinking that will cause everyone to believe in me. I could do it. But most often that's not God's plan. His plan is simple. He sent me to you, and I send you to others. Share my story person to person, life to life. You're a walking, talking example of me living in you.

Remember—it's not about you. No sales quotas or high pressure. I'm the one who lived the sinless life, died on the cross for the sins of the world, and defeated death. Keep the focus on my life, death, and resurrection. Avoid pointless arguments that go nowhere. Let them know you didn't deserve or earn grace and forgiveness. They are gifts from a loving God. Invite them to connect their lives with me as you did.

Keep it simple. Keep it real. The world is overloaded with crazy ideas that try to explain the meaning of life. When you tell my story using words others can understand, and they see authentic changes in your life, I will become real to them.

Not everyone will like you or your message. Some people will hate you (and me) when you talk about the good news. It can be discouraging. Keep on loving these people. Pray for them. God loves them as much he loves you!

But to the people who are seeking God, your life and message will be like the aroma of a delicious meal or the most wonderful perfume. Let me work through your life to reach your friends.

Love, Jesus

SUMMARY CHALLENGE: "Go into all the world and preach the Good News to everyone, everywhere." (Mark 16:15, NLT)

JOURNALING OPPORTUNITY:

DEVOTIONAL 24

The Best Feeling in the World

TOPIC: Joy

MAIN SCRIPTURE: "I have told you this so that you will be filled with my joy. Yes, your joy will overflow!" (John 15:11, NLT)

OTHER SCRIPTURES: Luke 10:20; Romans 14:7; 1 Peter 1:8

WHAT JESUS MIGHT SAY TO YOU:
What a winner you are! You have a reason to celebrate. God has given you more joy than a megamillion-dollar jackpot could ever give you. You have what no amount of money could ever buy. You are set for eternal life. You'll live forever—you don't have to fear death. Your life on earth is just the beginning. Your life with me will never end.

You are God's child—whatever you accomplish in life is nothing compared to your name being written in God's Book of Life. God's grace has already secured you the most important thing in life.

You have a brand-new life. In the past your life was full of darkness, but now it's full of light from me. You have a fresh start and a new outlook. Everything is possible. God helps you in everything—keep following me and doing what I would do, and the peace of God will be with you.

You know the truth—you were created to abide in me, to live connected to me. When you embrace me, obey me, and live in my love, your life will overflow with joy. Nobody and nothing can take that away from you.

Your joy, Jesus

SUMMARY CHALLENGE: Happiness depends on circumstances, but joy comes from knowing that God loves you. Can you find things to be joyful about today?

JOURNALING OPPORTUNITY:

DEVOTIONAL 25

Fearing for Your Life

TOPIC: Fear and trust

MAIN SCRIPTURES: "When I am afraid, I will trust in you." (Psalm 56:3)

"There is no fear in love. But perfect love drives out fear, because fear has to do with punishment. The one who fears is not made perfect in love." (1 John 4:18)

OTHER SCRIPTURES: Genesis 3:3-10; Exodus 16:16-20; Deuteronomy 1:31-33; Psalm 40:3-4; Luke 12:22-34; Philippians 4:6-7

WHAT JESUS MIGHT SAY TO YOU:

What are your fears? Rejection? Failure? Abandonment? Think about it. What are you afraid of? Why are you so afraid of these things?

In 1 John I tell you that my perfect love casts out all fear. So why are you still afraid? Maybe you need to trust me more, to learn to rest in my love?

Think about Adam and Eve. Satan convinced them that I was holding out on them...not giving them the absolute best. They stopped trusting me. They tried to get the best on their own by eating from the tree of knowledge. In the end they realized they should've trusted me. Adam's first words after his fall were, "I was afraid" (Genesis 3:10). Their fears led to doubt and inevitably more fear.

What about you? Do you think I'm holding out on you? That I won't come through? When you doubt these things, you'll be tempted to take control. Rather than surrendering to me and allowing me to rule in your heart, you will become ruled by your fears. You will become a slave to worry and lack of control. This is no way to live. It doesn't have to be this way. I'm bigger than all of your fears. Surrender them to me. Trust my love. It will extinguish your fears and set you free.

What are your fears keeping you from? How are they depriving you of life? Next time your doubt tempts you to take over, ask yourself, "How can I trust Jesus in this?" You have a choice to make. Trust my intentions toward you. I want the best for you and I will deliver. Stop struggling. Let me take care of you.

My love never fails, Jesus

SUMMARY CHALLENGE: Don't let your fears control you—instead trust Jesus.

JOURNALING OPPORTUNITY:

DEVOTIONAL 26

Life in Exile

TOPIC: Abundant life in the hard times

MAIN SCRIPTURES: "The LORD Almighty, the God of Israel, sends this message to all the captives he has exiled to Babylon from Jerusalem: 'Build homes, and plan to stay. Plant gardens, and eat the food you produce. Marry, and have children. Then find spouses for them, and have many grandchildren. Multiply! Do not dwindle away! And work for the peace and prosperity of Babylon. Pray to the LORD for that city where you are held captive, for if Babylon has peace, so will you.'" (Jeremiah 29:4-7, NLT)

"Those who plant in tears will harvest with shouts of joy. They weep as they go to plant their seed, but they sing as they return with the harvest." (Psalm 126:5-6, NLT)

OTHER SCRIPTURES: Psalm 126; Jeremiah 29:11-14; John 14:27

WHAT JESUS MIGHT SAY TO YOU:

Do you ever feel like you're living in a fog, like you don't know what's going on? Don't know where I'm leading you? Maybe you're living in a desert where you feel parched and nothing can grow, and you can't hear my voice? Do you want to know when it'll end?

It may be tempting just to curl up in a ball and shut out reality. But what if I told you it's actually possible to live the abundant life I have promised in the midst of these circumstances? The passages above describe the exile of the Israelites. They were banished from Jerusalem and forced to live in Babylon.

They were confused, frustrated, and suffering, and they wanted to go home. Pay close attention to my words for them.

I called them to carry on with life despite the circumstances... to plant gardens, have families, and invest in their surroundings. They wept and struggled to put roots down in this temporary place...but it was worth it, and it resulted in joy.

It's hard to carry on when you feel sad, frustrated, and confused. Pray for the desire to continue abiding in me, investing in others, and trusting my plans for you. For when you sow in tears, you will reap a harvest of joy. In the meantime know that I am with you, always faithful and devoted...giving you my peace, perseverance, and strength.

You may be desperately wondering when this dark period of your life will be over, but I'm asking you to trust me in the midst of it. I will be faithful. Whether I rescue you in seven days, seven years, or longer...you can have life and joy and love now. You can experience true life in the midst of your desert!

Your Oasis, Jesus

SUMMARY CHALLENGE: You don't have to wait for deliverance to live an abundant life.

JOURNALING OPPORTUNITY:

DEVOTIONAL 27

Overcoming the Beast Within

TOPIC: Lust

MAIN SCRIPTURE: "Those who live according to the sinful nature have their minds set on what that nature desires; but those who live in accordance with the Spirit have their minds set on what the Spirit desires." (Romans 8:5)

OTHER SCRIPTURES: Job 31:1; Proverbs 6:20-29; John 14:6; Romans 6-7; 1 Thessalonians 4:3-8; James 1:14-15; 1 Peter 2:11

WHAT JESUS MIGHT SAY TO YOU:

I know you ask yourself, "How can I ever overcome this enormous preoccupation with sex?" I also know that you ask yourself, "What's wrong with sex, anyway?" Sometimes it feels like a battle is being waged.

Right now I know that your hormones are raging, sexual images are assaulting you, and the pressure is increasing, like some animal inside you just pacing its cage.

But would you be surprised to know that I created you with that appetite? Sex is good. It's supposed to be really good. But it's not just some bodily function. It's part of my plan for your happiness. You were designed for the pleasure and fulfillment that comes within the intimate relationship of a man and a woman who are committed to one another for life.

In the meantime the animal inside you needs to remain in its cage. Allowing your sex drive to run free will only get you in trouble and drive you away from me. The battle to bring it under control begins with the influences around you. The TV shows and movies you watch and the music you listen to can feed the animal inside until it seems like it's going crazy, trying to break free from its cage. TV shows, movies, and music don't represent a realistic view of sex, anyway. You've been created as a sexual being, but remember: You are *more* than just a sexual being.

You become what you behold. In other words, if you focus your mind on sex, then sex will become the greatest focus (and obstacle) in your life. If you focus your mind solely on trying to overcome your lust, then sex will still be the focus (and greatest obstacle) in your life. But if you focus on me, you will become like me, and the beast won't be in control.

So run from temptation. Get rid of any influence that feeds the beast inside. And rather than indulging yourself in sex or obsessing on overcoming your problem with lust, indulge yourself in me. I know what you're going through.

Your Creator, Jesus

SUMMARY CHALLENGE: Indulge yourself in Christ, and you will become like Christ.

JOURNALING OPPORTUNITY:

DEVOTIONAL 28

The Power of Presence

TOPIC: Loving your hurting friends

MAIN SCRIPTURE: "Three of Job's friends were Eliphaz the Temanite, Bildad the Shuhite, and Zophar the Naamathite. When they heard of the tragedy he had suffered, they got together and traveled from their homes to comfort and console him. When they saw Job from a distance, they scarcely recognized him. Wailing loudly, they tore their robes and threw dust into the air over their heads to demonstrate their grief. Then they sat on the ground with him for seven days and nights. And no one said a word, for they saw that his suffering was too great for words." (Job 2:11-13, NLT)

OTHER SCRIPTURES: Job 13:4-5; Psalm 62:1-2; Proverbs 17:27-28; 2 Corinthians 1:4

WHAT JESUS MIGHT SAY TO YOU:
Your friends are hurting. How can you help? How can you comfort and encourage them in their times of need? What do you say? It's definitely not easy.

Please don't feel like you have to provide them with answers to solve their problems and ease their pain. Take some pointers from Job's three friends. Job suffered great tragedy and his friends responded. What did they do right? What did they do wrong?

When they first heard the news, they grieved deeply with Job. They simply sat with him in his despair for seven days. Later on they attempted to give Job some advice on the reasons and solutions for these tragedies. What was Job's response? He says, "You are merely useless doctors, who treat me with lies. The wisest thing you can do is to keep quiet" (Job 13:4-5, CEV). Oops. They should have stuck with their first response!

Does this ever happen to you—you try to help but make things worse? To sympathize you say, "I know how you feel," but your friend responds, "No, you don't. No one does!"

Answers are overrated—it's your presence that is powerful. Comfort your friend the way I comfort you (2 Corinthians 1:4). I hold you close and remind you of my love for you. This is more powerful than simply giving you a to-do list of solutions to fix pain. I am simply there with you and want you to rest in me. I am the only way to true hope and peace.

Comfort your friends. Be with them. Listen to them. Meet them where they're at. Do as I do. Whether they know me or not, you will be pointing them to me. Pain is a powerful doorway for my love.

Your Guide in comforting others, Jesus

SUMMARY CHALLENGE: Remember that your presence is more powerful than your words.

JOURNALING OPPORTUNITY:

DEVOTIONAL 29

Love Wins

TOPIC: It's about heart change, not "good morals"

MAIN SCRIPTURES: "Make a tree good and its fruit will be good, or make a tree bad and its fruit will be bad, for a tree is recognized by its fruit. You brood of vipers, how can you who are evil say anything good? For out of the overflow of the heart the mouth speaks. The good man brings good things out of the good stored up in him, and the evil man brings evil things out of the evil stored up in him." (Matthew 12:33-35)

"For if you confess with your mouth that Jesus is Lord and believe in your heart that God raised him from the dead, you will be saved. For it is by believing in your heart that you are made right with God, and it is by confessing with your mouth that you are saved." (Romans 10:9-10, NLT)

OTHER SCRIPTURES: Matthew 15:18-19; Mark 12:30-33; John 8:3-11

WHAT JESUS MIGHT SAY TO YOU:

Some Christians today believe that fixing a non-Christian's morals and behavior is the first step in introducing them to me. Not true! This leads to a dangerous "us versus them" mentality. Many of my followers believe that their morality makes them superior to the world. Sounds a lot like the Pharisees, doesn't it?

This is not my way. The last thing people want to hear is how you think they should act or think. People don't respond positively to this, and besides, morals don't save you. My Word says that a person's actions reveal her heart. The heart is where problems reside. Poor choices are merely symptoms. You don't heal the flu by stopping a sneeze.

Changed behavior is the result of a changed heart. Rules don't change hearts. Only love changes hearts. This is my way. This is what I died for.

If you want someone to know me truly, my love must be your motive and your message. Focus on the internal, not the external. Rather than condemning them, listen to them. Understand their hearts and where they're coming from. Focus on their needs and their desires in light of my grace, my forgiveness, and my unconditional love.

I'll meet them exactly where they are. I am what their hearts have been searching for. When they find fulfillment in me, they'll stop seeking it elsewhere. Their choices will change. Because the concepts of right and wrong don't motivate change. Judgment certainly doesn't motivate change. Relationships motivate change. Love motivates change. This is my message. I am *for* people, not against them.

My message is simple: Love me and love others. When you do, you will see the world change...one life at a time.

My love is greater than any law, Jesus

SUMMARY CHALLENGE: When sharing Jesus, love goes further than condemnation.

JOURNALING OPPORTUNITY:

DEVOTIONAL 30

Your Reservations Are Confirmed

TOPIC: Feeling scared about death

MAIN SCRIPTURE: "For to me, living means opportunities for Christ, and dying—well, that's better yet." (Philippians 1:21, Living Bible)

OTHER SCRIPTURES: John 14:1-6; 1 Corinthians 15:12-23; Philippians 1:21-24

WHAT JESUS MIGHT SAY TO YOU:

Tell me what scares you about death. It terrifies most people who talk to me. In fact, when death is nearby, people start talking to me like crazy. People I haven't heard from in years immediately want my attention.

You know my story, right? I was killed when I lived in my human body on earth. It wasn't pretty. I died a horrible death and experienced unbelievable pain. The worst part was the separation from God (my Father) that I experienced when I took on the sin of the whole world (yours included). I was still me. I had absolute power that day. At any point I could've turned away from that horror, but I went the whole way to break death's hold on you so you wouldn't have to be afraid of death. I did what no other "religious leader" ever did. I died and came back to life—and I'm still alive. I'm talking to you every day through the Holy Spirit.

Thomas, my famous doubting disciple, was scared about being separated from me when I died. I told him I was going ahead to prepare a place for him (and you). That place is real and waiting for you when your life on earth is over. Thomas even wanted directions on how to get there. I told him (and you, too) that I am the Way, the Truth, and the Life (John 14:6). No one can come to God the Father except through me. Put your faith and trust in me, and you secure a place with me in heaven forever. It's all paid for by my death and guaranteed by my resurrection. So when you die, you have no reason to be afraid.

When your friends talk about death, let them know I've shown you the way to heaven. Tell them my story. They have nothing to fear.

Waiting for you, Jesus

SUMMARY CHALLENGE: "When I am afraid, I will put my trust in You." (Psalm 56:3, NASB)

JOURNALING OPPORTUNITY:

DEVOTIONAL 31

Life Outside the Bubble

TOPIC: Get out of your comfort zone

MAIN SCRIPTURES: "But how can they call on him to save them unless they believe in him? And how can they believe in him if they have never heard about him? And how can they hear about him unless someone tells them? And how will anyone go and tell them without being sent? That is what the Scriptures mean when they say, 'How beautiful are the feet of those who bring good news!'" (Romans 10:14-15, NLT)

"We proclaim Him, admonishing every man and teaching every man with all wisdom, so that we may present every man complete in Christ. For this purpose also I labor, striving according to His power, which mightily works within me." (Colossians 1:28-29, NASB)

OTHER SCRIPTURES: Jeremiah 20:9; Mark 16:15; John 17:16,18; Colossians 4:5-7; 1 John 3:18

WHAT JESUS MIGHT SAY TO YOU:

Step back for a moment. Take a look at your life. Is it mostly a routine? Are you stuck in a bubble, afraid to step outside your comfort zone? Do you always hang out with the same people, mostly people like you?

If so, I want to share something with you: I want to pop the bubble you live in, get you out of your comfort zone. Why? For others. Because I love the world you live in. I want others to know me. I died for them, too. Because I chose you to be my representative to them, I have called you to go. Because they won't know unless someone tells them. What if someone had not told you? Because...how will this world change unless you change it?

For you: Because growth does not occur in the comfort zone. Because I want you to listen for my voice and trust me enough to obey. Because I want you to learn to love boldly and step out on a limb for the sake of others. Because you can't fully experience my love unless you share it with others.

What changes can you make? Think about how you can make time in your life to invest in others. Don't let Satan tell you that you're too busy and can't do it. I am the author of time. Don't wait for others to come to you. Go to them. Love is active. Encourage them. Take them to coffee. Go eat lunch with them. Who am I placing on your heart? I would not put them there without great purpose. Trust me.

In love I am calling you to leave your bubble. There's a whole world waiting for you.

With hope for the world, Jesus

SUMMARY CHALLENGE: Living a life of love requires leaving your comfort zone.

JOURNALING OPPORTUNITY:

DEVOTIONAL 32

Suffering Can Serve You

TOPIC: Dealing with loss

MAIN SCRIPTURE: "My grace is sufficient for you, for my power is made perfect in weakness." (2 Corinthians 12:9, ESV)

OTHER SCRIPTURES: Psalm 61:1-4; Psalm 62:1-2; Matthew 27:45-46; Mark 15:34

WHAT JESUS MIGHT SAY TO YOU:

When was the last time you felt the loss of someone or something really important? Where do you turn when you can't feel or see even me?

Listen, my child, I am present for you, strong and ready to save you right now. My grace is sufficient for you. My power is made perfect in weakness. Your loss of friendship, your loss of love, your loss of victory, your fear of losing more—all of the suffering you feel through loss—all of it can serve you. I make all things new. I will rescue you. I am your strength and your song.

All my followers suffer loss sometimes. What happens after your loss often determines how our relationship grows. Protect yourself from becoming bitter by drawing near to me even when you feel angry or abandoned. Ask me to carry this burden with you...and always wait for me to answer.

I am not slow to answer. Sometimes, however, I wait for you to wait for me, and then I respond. Other times I respond before you even ask. All I ask is that you ask, wait, abide.

You are my delight. You are my joy. When you suffer from loss, abide in my love; allow our two stories to merge together so that you are never alone. As I write the story of your life, our stories intersect every time you lean into my love, every time you trust me, every time you wait for me.

My child, I am carrying the loss with you. My friend, I am here for you. My love, I am always right next to you.

Your Protector, Jesus

SUMMARY CHALLENGE: Fear not—Jesus suffers with you.

JOURNALING OPPORTUNITY:

DEVOTIONAL 33

The Opposition

TOPIC: Understanding the Enemy's schemes

MAIN SCRIPTURES: "Be careful! Watch out for attacks from the Devil, your great enemy. He prowls around like a roaring lion, looking for some victim to devour. Take a firm stand against him, and be strong in your faith. Remember that your Christian brothers and sisters all over the world are going through the same kind of suffering you are." (1 Peter 5:8-9, NLT)

"He was a murderer from the beginning and has always hated the truth. There is no truth in him. When he lies, it is consistent with his character; for he is a liar and the father of lies." (John 8:44, NLT)

OTHER SCRIPTURES: Psalm 143:3-4; John 10:10; Acts 10:38; 2 Corinthians 2:11; 2 Corinthians 11:14; 1 John 3:8; Revelation 12:17

WHAT JESUS MIGHT SAY TO YOU:
Satan will press you...he knows exactly which buttons to push. He'll do anything to keep you from all that is worthy of your attention. He will attack your heart, the core of who you are. If anything is good or beautiful or life-giving, he'll try to take it from you. Why? Because he's afraid of you. He knows exactly who I have created you to be. You're a threat to him!

Please understand how Satan works. His schemes may seem complex and twisted, but they're actually quite childish and simple. He is just waving his arms around, shouting, "Look over here!" to distract you, scare you, and get you to take your eyes off me. He'll do anything to keep you from the unfathomable love and great adventure I have for you.

He knows your weaknesses and insecurities. Does this sound familiar? "I can't do that because..." or "I'm terrible at this..." or "They're trying to hurt my feelings..." or "I'm not good enough," etc.? Do NOT listen or agree! That's Satan! He strikes at the very core of your emotions, your insecurities, your identity.

Never respond by giving him your time or attention. Recognize the lies. Turn your eyes back to me. Remember who you are, who I made you to be. Don't let him fool you. I will help you fight! We have already won the war. We can take him.

Your Defender, Jesus

SUMMARY CHALLENGE: Keep your eyes open...don't let Satan get the best of you.

JOURNALING OPPORTUNITY:

Jesus Has Faith in Us

TOPIC: Jesus has faith in us

MAIN SCRIPTURES: "I tell you the truth, anyone who has faith in me will do what I have been doing. He will do even greater things than these, because I am going to the Father." (John 14:12)

"When they saw the courage of Peter and John and realized that they were unschooled, ordinary men, they were astonished and they took note that these men had been with Jesus." (Acts 4:13)

OTHER SCRIPTURES: Matthew 16:18-19; Matthew 17:20; John 21:15-17; Acts 1:8; Ephesians 1:11-12, 19-20

WHAT JESUS MIGHT SAY TO YOU:
Have you read my words to you in John 14:12? Do you understand what they mean? If so, you're probably feeling overwhelmed, right? "How on earth can I do greater things than Jesus, let alone the same things? I can't even get my own life together!"

I understand your feelings, and I want to encourage you.

Believe it or not, I chose you—to follow me...to be my friend and child...but also to be my coworker. I have faith in you. You're usually taught to have faith in me, but I'm telling you that I also have great faith in you. I would not have chosen you if I did not believe you could do what I do. I returned to heaven knowing that you're able to continue my work.

Look at the men I chose for disciples. They were unschooled... and not successful, well-respected, or powerful men. But they became powerful because I worked through them. Although Peter denied me three times, I chose him to feed my sheep and build my church.

Being my disciple means following me closely, learning from me, becoming like me, and doing what I do. This is what it means to abide. We become inseparable. As my child, you also have the Holy Spirit. You have God dwelling in you, giving you the ability to be like me and move mountains!

Don't underestimate yourself and who I've made you to be. When you are weak, I am strong. You are made in my image and filled with my Spirit...by whom you have access to the same power that raised me from the dead! You can be like me. I have faith in you. Trust me as I trust you.

Go...and be my disciple.

Follow my lead, Jesus

SUMMARY CHALLENGE: Jesus has faith in you; he believes you can be like him.

JOURNALING OPPORTUNITY:

DEVOTIONAL 35

The Benefits of Brokenness

TOPIC: Brokenness—our friends' and ours

MAIN SCRIPTURES: "He comforts us in all our troubles so that we can comfort others. When others are troubled, we will be able to give them the same comfort God has given us." (2 Corinthians 1:4, NLT)

"This is real love. It is not that we loved God, but that he loved us and sent his Son as a sacrifice to take away our sins. Dear friends, since God loved us that much, we surely ought to love each other." (1 John 4:10-11, NLT)

OTHER SCRIPTURES: Psalm 147:3; Matthew 9:11-13; Romans 7:15,19-20; 2 Corinthians 12:9

WHAT JESUS MIGHT SAY TO YOU:

"I wish my phone would ring more often...I don't know how to fit in...I only feel beautiful when I'm hungry...I listen to my friends, but no one listens to me...."

Do you recognize these voices? They're the voices of your peers. They're hurting, broken. They need me. What about you? Do you ever feel this way? Probably. That's because you still need me...every...single...day.

What have you been forgiven for? Why do you still need me every day? What are you struggling with right now?

That's right...you and your peers are all in the same mess whether they know me or not. You're all struggling, hurting, in need of grace...in need of me—sheep that need a shepherd.

I want you to understand two things: One—I am the answer for your brokenness. Me, not some to-do list. My love meets you in your brokenness and moves you toward wholeness. Life without me is hollow. I fulfill you. I restore you. I show you the real life you were created to live. Two—I want to use you in your brokenness. How? Brokenness enables you to profoundly experience my love and your need for me. This allows us to go deep. This will help you relate to your peers and better understand their needs. Then you can share with them the very love I've shown you. You have a role in others' brokenness. I am the answer for your brokenness. My followers and I are the answer for the world's brokenness.

You understand need because you have need. You're able to love because I first loved you. Get connected to others' lives, meet them in their need...then show them the love, hope, and healing you've found in me. They're waiting.

Your Healer, Jesus

SUMMARY CHALLENGE: Jesus wants to use your brokenness in others' lives.

JOURNALING OPPORTUNITY:

DEVOTIONAL 36

Are You for Real?

TOPIC: Being real

MAIN SCRIPTURES: "We loved you so much that we gave you not only God's Good News but our own lives, too." (1 Thessalonians 2:8, NLT)

"If we claim to be without sin, we deceive ourselves and the truth is not in us. If we confess our sins, he is faithful and just and will forgive us our sins and purify us from all unrighteousness." (1 John 1:8-9)

OTHER SCRIPTURES: Matthew 7:4-5; 1 Corinthians 9:22-23; Philippians 3:7-8; Philippians 4:12-14

WHAT JESUS MIGHT SAY TO YOU:

Do you ever find yourself pretending you have it all together? Why? Do you think you're poorly representing me if your imperfections show? Are you afraid that people will discover your secrets? This is dangerous. Why? Because it's fake. You're not fooling anyone. I hear the thoughts of many people who are tired of Christians wearing masks, tired of hypocrisy. They want the real deal.

Why is it so necessary to be real?

First, for your relationship with me. If you're not being vulnerable with me, then you're not fully letting me into your heart. How can I help if you don't let me in? How will you experience my grace and love? Be assured: There's nothing hiding in your heart that'll make me love you any less. I want you to heal and be whole.

Second, for your relationships with others. People most effectively see the beauty of my love when they can see me working in your life. This is your story. This is how they'll catch a glimpse of my grace. If you had it all together, you wouldn't need me. They won't understand their need for me unless they see your need for me.

Being real means admitting you don't have it together. Don't worry about others' opinions. You have nothing to prove. Your worth comes from me. People will gain respect for you when you're honest. They will open up when they know you can relate.

My love seeks you out, no matter where you're at or where you've been. You don't have to clean yourself up before you come to me. That is my gospel. Communicate it with your life. There's no reason to hide...and every reason to step into the light.

Your reputation, Jesus

SUMMARY CHALLENGE: Get real. Your friends will thank you for it!

JOURNALING OPPORTUNITY:

DEVOTIONAL 37

Love Doesn't Come Easily

TOPIC: Loving others even when it's hard

MAIN SCRIPTURE: "Be imitators of God, therefore, as dearly loved children and live a life of love, just as Christ loved us and gave himself up for us as a fragrant offering and sacrifice to God." (Ephesians 5:1-2)

OTHER SCRIPTURES: Matthew 5:46-48; John 15:9; John 15:12; 1 John 3:18

WHAT JESUS MIGHT SAY TO YOU:

It's hard to love people sometimes, isn't it? Why is that? Could it be because your love may not be returned or because their response doesn't benefit you or make you feel valued?

Here's the bad news: Love is hard. The good news is: I can help.

Think of how often people reject my love. It breaks my heart every single time...but I keep on loving them. Think of all the times you've disregarded me and chosen your own way. Even then I kept on loving you, no matter what.

Now I ask you to love others in this same way. My love will enable you to do this. My love is not dependent on outcome. True love is sacrificial. There's a cost. I gave my life because I love you. Love others because of me and as an offering to me, not because of what you anticipate in return. Love others the way I love you.

Don't let someone's response to your love determine your identity or self-worth. Let me determine your value. Be secure and content in my love. My love for you will never change. Let me be your anchor.

Love others for my sake and in my name. It will be hard, but it will be worth the struggle.

Let your love for others be unwavering, just like my love for you. Do not be shaken. Make me your first love. When this happens, my love will overflow to others through you. My love changes lives!

Let my love be your motivation and your strength.

Your Source, Jesus

SUMMARY CHALLENGE: Let Jesus' love for you motivate you to love others, even when it's hard.

JOURNALING OPPORTUNITY:

DEVOTIONAL 38

For a High-Mileage Heart

TOPIC: Caring for your heart

MAIN SCRIPTURE: "Above all else, guard your heart, for it affects everything you do." (Proverbs 4:23, NLT)

OTHER SCRIPTURES: Psalm 51:10; Psalm 61:2; Mark 12:30; 2 Corinthians 4:16-17; Ephesians 1:18-19

WHAT JESUS MIGHT SAY TO YOU:

Your heart is the core of who you are. It is precious, the center of your relationship with me. It's how you're able to love others. Everything depends on it. You cannot love if you have nothing to give.

This is why I want you to guard your heart. "Guard" does not mean locking it up and keeping it prisoner. It means watching over it...caring for it...keeping it healthy.

Satan aims for your heart. He keeps you so busy that you ignore it. A tired, run-down heart is vulnerable. It won't take much to take you out. I want your heart to be strong so that it's resilient against Satan, but also so it can be full to the point of overflowing.

Do you consciously care for your heart? What do you do to care for your heart? What could you be doing?

Spending time with me is the best way to care for your heart. I understand that it can be difficult to put effort into reading my Word and praying when your heart is tired. So let's think of some other ways to spend time together.

What do you love to do? What helps you escape? Painting? Music? Photography? Sports? Reading? Being outdoors? I have given you these passions for a reason. They bring you joy. They feel like rewards rather than chores. When your heart needs refreshment, do what you love. And then use those things to hang out with me. Invite me into your joy.

Think about some other things you can do to care for your heart. Life is too short for your heart to be captive to obligations. I want you to live an abundant life...and you're going to need your heart.

Filling you to overflowing, Jesus

SUMMARY CHALLENGE: Take good care of your heart—you need it.

JOURNALING OPPORTUNITY:

DEVOTIONAL 39

Stay Tuned

TOPIC: Listening to the voice of the Spirit

MAIN SCRIPTURES: "As for Philip, an angel of the Lord said to him, 'Go south down the desert road that runs from Jerusalem to Gaza.' So he did, and he met the treasurer of Ethiopia, a eunuch of great authority under the queen of Ethiopia. The eunuch had gone to Jerusalem to worship, and he was now returning. Seated in his carriage, he was reading aloud from the book of the prophet Isaiah. The Holy Spirit said to Philip, 'Go over and walk along beside the carriage.' Philip ran over and heard the man reading from the prophet Isaiah; so he asked, 'Do you understand what you are reading?' The man replied, 'How can I, when there is no one to instruct me?' And he begged Philip to come up into the carriage and sit with him...So Philip began with this same Scripture and then used many others to tell him the Good News about Jesus. As they rode along, they came to some water, and the eunuch said, 'Look! There's some water! Why can't I be baptized?' He ordered the carriage to stop, and they went down into the water, and Philip baptized him. When they came up out of the water, the Spirit of the Lord caught Philip away. The eunuch never saw him again but went on his way rejoicing. Meanwhile, Philip found himself farther north at the city of Azotus! He preached the Good News there and in every city along the way until he came to Caesarea." (Acts 8:26-31, 35-40, NLT)

"And now, compelled by the Spirit, I am going to Jerusalem, not knowing what will happen to me there." (Acts 20:22)

OTHER SCRIPTURES: Matthew 10:19-20; Acts 1:8; Acts 13:2-3; Acts 16:6-10; Acts 18:9-11

WHAT JESUS MIGHT SAY TO YOU:
Have you ever felt my Spirit prompting you to do something? Did you do it? If not, why not? Were you afraid of the unknown? Too

shy? Embarrassed? I understand your feelings. It's hard to take a step of faith into the unknown. Here's some encouragement.

Look at the story of Philip above. My Spirit told him to walk 50 miles into the desert. And he went, no questions asked. If I had told him what was awaiting him that day, he would've been overwhelmed...but I led him one small step at a time. He trusted me, and I was faithful. And look how I used him. Because of Philip's obedience, that Ethiopian found hope and a new relationship with me.

Believe it or not, this still happens today. It happens when I choose to use ordinary people like you to do extraordinary things. They listen. They hear. They follow.

Don't be afraid to follow my Spirit's leading. It's like a scavenger hunt. My Spirit will guide you and give you each next step as you need it. Your only role is to obey. I know the outcome even if you don't. Look at my track record in Scripture. I'm faithful. I prepared these things for you before you were even born. You can trust me. I won't let you fail.

If I send you, I'll get you there. If I call you to speak, I'll give you the words. I will take care of you. When you feel the tug of my Spirit and follow, you'll be amazed at what you see me do. But you have to be listening for it. You will experience more of me than you ever thought possible!

Tuned in, Jesus

SUMMARY CHALLENGE: Follow the Spirit, one step at a time, and you'll be amazed where you end up.

JOURNALING OPPORTUNITY:

DEVOTIONAL 40

The Story You Live In

TOPIC: Living a heroic life

MAIN SCRIPTURES: "Therefore I, a prisoner for serving the Lord, beg you to lead a life worthy of your calling, for you have been called by God." (Ephesians 4:1, NLT)

"Then make me truly happy by agreeing wholeheartedly with each other, loving one another, and working together with one heart and purpose. Don't be selfish; don't live to make a good impression on others. Be humble, thinking of others as better than yourself. Don't think only about your own affairs, but be interested in others, too, and what they are doing. Your attitude should be the same that Christ Jesus had. Though he was God, he did not demand and cling to his rights as God. He made himself nothing; he took the humble position of a slave and appeared in human form. And in human form he obediently humbled himself even further by dying a criminal's death on a cross." Philippians 2:2-8 (NLT)

OTHER SCRIPTURES: Mark 8:35-36; Mark 10:45; John 17:9-23; Acts 20:24-27; Romans 8:18-27; Galatians 6:9; Philippians 3:13-14; 1 Peter 4:10

WHAT JESUS MIGHT SAY TO YOU:
Your generation is special. You live in a unique time. You are socially aware. You want to be heroes. You want to serve, to be part of something bigger than yourselves. You're activists. You're unhappy with the state of the world and you want to do something about it. Considering the world you live in, this is absolutely necessary.

Whether you realize it or not, you are playing a role in a much larger story, a story of redemption. I am Yahweh, the One who is, who was, and is to come. I am doing, I have done, and I will do whatever it takes to reclaim my creation from the fall— from Satan. This began before the Father sent me into the world to be crucified and resurrected, to redeem my children. My birth was an act of war. When I return a second time, I will complete my plan of redemption. The rescue will be complete.

You live in the in-between time, and believe it or not, you have a part to play in this great story. What is your role? To fight alongside me—by loving, by serving. Maybe even at your own expense. Putting yourself aside for the benefit of others, just like I've done.

Whether it's children dying of AIDS in Africa or the girl in math who's suffering a broken heart...you can make a difference. I have called you to care for those who cannot care for themselves. You're able to do so because my love flows through you as you abide in me.

This is the world you live in, but this is not your home. Do not be caught up in things that will only serve you and last for this lifetime. Put others first and make a difference that will last for eternity. What impact will your generation make for my name?

Your Servant Savior, Jesus

SUMMARY CHALLENGE: This world is hurting and this life is short—what will you do?

JOURNALING OPPORTUNITY:

DEVOTIONAL 41

Walk in the Truth

TOPIC: Putting on the belt of truth

MAIN SCRIPTURE: "Use every piece of God's armor to resist the enemy in the time of evil, so that after the battle you will still be standing firm. Stand your ground, putting on the sturdy belt of truth and the body armor of God's righteousness. For shoes, put on the peace that comes from the Good News, so that you will be fully prepared. In every battle you will need faith as your shield to stop the fiery arrows aimed at you by Satan. Put on salvation as your helmet, and take the sword of the Spirit, which is the word of God. Pray at all times and on every occasion in the power of the Holy Spirit. Stay alert and be persistent in your prayers for all Christians everywhere." (Ephesians 6:13-18, NLT)

OTHER SCRIPTURES: Isaiah 11:5; John 3:21; John 14:6; 2 Corinthians 1:12; Ephesians 4:15, 25; 1 John 1:5-10

WHAT JESUS MIGHT SAY TO YOU:

I know that you constantly face the temptation to live by deception. You can take a test at school that reflects your study habits, or you can cheat. You can live as the person you really are inside, or you can try to act a certain way so that certain people will approve of you. You can suffer the consequences of your choices, or you can lie to your parents to keep from getting in trouble.

Living by deception may seem easier than walking in the truth, but it isn't better—for you or our friendship.

Truth is a crucial component of the protection God provides for your soul in this world. I encourage you to wrap yourself in it.

Speak truth (in love, of course). Seek truth. Live in the truth. Love truth. Walk in truth. Truth isn't just a concept—truth is a person. I am that person. I am the Way, the Truth, and the Life.

Living in truth isn't easy. It may mean studying harder at school, scoring lower on the cool quotient, or spending the occasional weekend without anything "fun" to do. But you'll discover a peace that living by deception can never offer. When you live by deception, you live in the fear of being caught, of being found out for who you really are.

So be who you are. Be a lover and seeker of truth, and you'll discover that you are a lover and seeker of me. Because when you put on the belt of truth, you put on me.

Your Truth, Jesus

SUMMARY CHALLENGE: Love, live, and seek truth.

JOURNALING OPPORTUNITY:

DEVOTIONAL 42

Looking in the Mirror and Seeing Jesus

TOPIC: Putting on the breastplate of righteousness

MAIN SCRIPTURE: "Use every piece of God's armor to resist the enemy in the time of evil, so that after the battle you will still be standing firm. Stand your ground, putting on the sturdy belt of truth and the body armor of God's righteousness. For shoes, put on the peace that comes from the Good News, so that you will be fully prepared. In every battle you will need faith as your shield to stop the fiery arrows aimed at you by Satan. Put on salvation as your helmet, and take the sword of the Spirit, which is the word of God. Pray at all times and on every occasion in the power of the Holy Spirit. Stay alert and be persistent in your prayers for all Christians everywhere." (Ephesians 6:13-18, NLT)

OTHER SCRIPTURES: Isaiah 11:5; Isaiah 59:17; Isaiah 61:10-11; Jeremiah 23:6; Romans 3:21-26; 1 Corinthians 1:30-31; 2 Corinthians 5:17-21; Philippians 3:7-11; Titus 3:4-8

WHAT JESUS MIGHT SAY TO YOU:
When you look in the mirror, what do you see? A screwup? An underachiever? Someone who's too ugly, too skinny, too fat, or too dumb?

Do you know how I see you? I see you as perfect. I know you think otherwise, and we both know that you still struggle with sin, but I've covered you with my righteousness. When you give your life to me, I cover your imperfection with my perfection...your sin with my cleansing blood. And when my Father in heaven sees you, he sees you through me. That's what it means to be covered with my righteousness.

You no longer have to be good enough to win my Father's approval. You already have it. You no longer have to feel the pressure of living up to God's standard because I am your standard. I am your righteousness. Your forgiveness. Your perfection.

When you look in the mirror, put on your body armor, your breastplate of righteousness. The chief purpose of body armor is to protect your internal organs, especially your heart. Every time you believe the lies of Satan, the Enemy of your soul, and you criticize yourself or define yourself by your actions, you allow damage to your heart.

When you put on the breastplate of righteousness, you put on me. So remind your heart that what you see and what you do don't define who you are. Your value doesn't depend on how much or how little you sin. Your value comes solely from me.

But don't get me wrong: That doesn't mean you can live for yourself. Your righteousness cost me my life. If you're grateful for receiving this gift, then let me live my life through you.

Your Righteousness, Jesus

SUMMARY CHALLENGE: When you look at yourself in the mirror, evaluate yourself as if you were talking about Jesus.

JOURNALING OPPORTUNITY:

DEVOTIONAL 43

Don't Just Know It...
Live It

TOPIC: Shoes of the gospel of peace

MAIN SCRIPTURE: "Use every piece of God's armor to resist the enemy in the time of evil, so that after the battle you will still be standing firm. Stand your ground, putting on the sturdy belt of truth and the body armor of God's righteousness. For shoes, put on the peace that comes from the Good News, so that you will be fully prepared. In every battle you will need faith as your shield to stop the fiery arrows aimed at you by Satan. Put on salvation as your helmet, and take the sword of the Spirit, which is the word of God. Pray at all times and on every occasion in the power of the Holy Spirit. Stay alert and be persistent in your prayers for all Christians everywhere." (Ephesians 6:13-18, NLT)

OTHER SCRIPTURES: Matthew 7:24-27; Romans 5:1-5; Romans 10:14-17; Ephesians 2:14; 2 Timothy 2:22; James 1:22-25; 1 Peter 3:8-12

WHAT JESUS MIGHT SAY TO YOU:
I hear your thoughts when you sit in class at school and ask yourself, "What does this have to do with the real world?" Facts trapped in your head that don't affect your everyday life do you little good.

The same is true of my Word and me. Rather than allow your knowledge of me to stay in your head, let it penetrate your heart and flow throughout your body. Your faith in me does you no good unless it affects your everyday life.

My heart breaks when I see you facing battles against Satan that knock you off your feet. You need the firm footing that comes from putting your faith into practice.

In the same way you put on a pair of shoes, put on the peace that comes from the good news so that you will be prepared for any situation. My good news becomes peace to you when you know deep inside that it's true. And you know it's true when it has become real in your life.

What does this mean for you? It means allowing me to become real in you. Let me live in you. Let me live through you. I am your peace. I am the good news. I am the real world.

Talk about my love, but love the people I place in your life, too—even those you may view as unlovable. Believe in my power but also believe that I have the power to change your seemingly unchangeable situation. Be thankful for the patience I show you but also show patience to people who get on your nerves.

When you experience the peace that comes from knowing that the good news is true, you not only prepare yourself to withstand any attack, but you also put on...me.

Your Peace, Jesus

SUMMARY CHALLENGE: Put your faith into practice so that when you face an overwhelming spiritual battle, you're standing on the solid ground that comes from knowing deep inside that the good news is true.

JOURNALING OPPORTUNITY:

DEVOTIONAL 44

Protection from Temptation

TOPIC: Putting on the shield of faith

MAIN SCRIPTURE: "Use every piece of God's armor to resist the enemy in the time of evil, so that after the battle you will still be standing firm. Stand your ground, putting on the sturdy belt of truth and the body armor of God's righteousness. For shoes, put on the peace that comes from the Good News, so that you will be fully prepared. In every battle you will need faith as your shield to stop the fiery arrows aimed at you by Satan. Put on salvation as your helmet, and take the sword of the Spirit, which is the word of God. Pray at all times and on every occasion in the power of the Holy Spirit. Stay alert and be persistent in your prayers for all Christians everywhere." (Ephesians 6:13-18, NLT)

OTHER SCRIPTURES: Psalm 18; Psalm 28:7; Proverbs 18:10; Isaiah 42:3; Romans 8:31-39; 1 Corinthians 10:13; Ephesians 2:8-9; 1 Thessalonians 5:8; Hebrews 11; 1 Peter 5:8-9; 1 John 5:4-5

WHAT JESUS MIGHT SAY TO YOU:
Do you remember when you were younger and cried out for protection from someone intent on hurting you? What you needed was a protector, a shield from Satan's attack.

Now that you're older, the dangers you face go much deeper than the threat of physical pain. Every day you encounter temptations that are like poisonous arrows aimed at your soul—arrows that deaden your conscience, rob your innocence, and harden your heart toward me; arrows of doubt, despair, compromise, and selfishness.

I know you feel overwhelmed by the pressure to conform to the standards of this world. But how do you withstand these attacks on your soul?

Lift up your shield of faith. I'm your shield. Your shelter. Your strong tower. Your protector. Place your faith in my power to help you. Call out to me, and I will make a way through any firestorm of temptation. Without me you can't overcome, but with me you are more than a conqueror.

Nothing can touch you except what comes through me—because I'm in control. You may seem overwhelmed by the temptations you're facing, but trust me—I won't let anything happen to you that you can't handle.

So cry out to me and look to me for help because I long to rescue you. And know that when you lift up your shield of faith, you lift up me.

Your Shield, Jesus

SUMMARY CHALLENGE: Call out to Jesus, and he will make a way through any firestorm of temptation.

JOURNALING OPPORTUNITY:

DEVOTIONAL 45

It's All about Him

TOPIC: Putting on the helmet of salvation

MAIN SCRIPTURE: "Use every piece of God's armor to resist the enemy in the time of evil, so that after the battle you will still be standing firm. Stand your ground, putting on the sturdy belt of truth and the body armor of God's righteousness. For shoes, put on the peace that comes from the Good News, so that you will be fully prepared. In every battle you will need faith as your shield to stop the fiery arrows aimed at you by Satan. Put on salvation as your helmet, and take the sword of the Spirit, which is the word of God. Pray at all times and on every occasion in the power of the Holy Spirit. Stay alert and be persistent in your prayers for all Christians everywhere." (Ephesians 6:13-18, NLT)

OTHER SCRIPTURES: Deuteronomy 31:8; Psalm 27:1; Isaiah 59:17; Isaiah 61:10; Ephesians 1:3-14; Colossians 1:15-20; Colossians 3:1-4; 1 Thessalonians 5:8

WHAT JESUS MIGHT SAY TO YOU:
It's all about me. No, really. You wouldn't exist if I hadn't created you. You wouldn't know me if I hadn't made myself known to you first. And you wouldn't be able to receive the gift of eternal life if I hadn't died on the cross for your sins. I am your salvation.

It works to your advantage that it's all about me. If life were all about you, then your salvation would depend on you. You would spend the rest of your life earning the right to spend eternity with me. You would live in fear of never measuring up and maybe not going to heaven after you die. But all you need to do—all you can do—is put on the helmet of salvation...*my* salvation.

Satan will do whatever he can to convince you that your salvation is all about you. But by putting on the helmet of salvation, you protect yourself from his assaults.

When you mess up, trust in the power of my blood to cleanse you from the stain of sin. When you doubt if you'll ever be good enough, trust in my good work on the cross to save you. When you're afraid that you've strayed too far to find your way back home, trust in my promise that I will never leave you nor forsake you.

So stop trying to be good enough. Stop beating yourself up. Stop worrying about the possibility of losing your salvation. Put on the helmet of salvation and trust that you will spend eternity with me not because of the good or bad things you've done, but because of what I've done for you. And know this: By putting on the helmet of salvation, you are putting on me.

Your Salvation, Jesus

SUMMARY CHALLENGE: Trust that Jesus' death on the cross is your only salvation—not your good or sinful actions.

JOURNALING OPPORTUNITY:

DEVOTIONAL 46

Your Only Weapon

TOPIC: Using the sword of the Spirit

MAIN SCRIPTURE: "Use every piece of God's armor to resist the enemy in the time of evil, so that after the battle you will still be standing firm. Stand your ground, putting on the sturdy belt of truth and the body armor of God's righteousness. For shoes, put on the peace that comes from the Good News, so that you will be fully prepared. In every battle you will need faith as your shield to stop the fiery arrows aimed at you by Satan. Put on salvation as your helmet, and take the sword of the Spirit, which is the word of God. Pray at all times and on every occasion in the power of the Holy Spirit. Stay alert and be persistent in your prayers for all Christians everywhere." (Ephesians 6:13-18, NLT)

OTHER SCRIPTURES: Psalm 119:11; Isaiah 40:8; Luke 4:1-12; John 1:14; Hebrews 4:12-13; Revelation 1:16; Revelation 12:11; Revelation 19:15

WHAT JESUS MIGHT SAY TO YOU:
Every day our relationship faces continuous attacks from Satan. Through greed, selfishness, dishonesty, sexual compromise, and a host of other sins, Satan is intent on destroying our relationship.

In your battle against Satan and the forces of evil, I have given you one weapon to strike back with: The sword of the Spirit, which is the Word of God.

At my weakest point during my time on earth, Satan tempted me to sacrifice everything for a shortcut to power, fame, and provision. And believe me, the temptation was great. But in that moment I pulled out my sword of the Spirit and struck back.

Rather than rely on profound arguments or scientific proofs, I quoted the Word of God.

When you face temptation in your greatest moment of weakness...when your friends or your teachers attack our relationship...when you face discouragement and despair that make you wonder if life is worth living...strike back with the sword of the Spirit. Be careful not to use it to hurt or demean others, but rely on it as your primary resource in responding to whatever attacks you encounter—whether they come directly from Satan or through people around you.

When you spend time in my Word, you also spend time with me because I am God's Word in human form.

So lift up the sword of the Spirit and know that when you do, you also lift me up.

Your Sword, Jesus

SUMMARY CHALLENGE: Immerse yourself in God's Word: Read it, learn it, understand it, and apply it to your life. No power on earth can stand against the eternal Word of God.

JOURNALING OPPORTUNITY:

DEVOTIONAL 47

Dance with Me

TOPIC: Not trusting God

MAIN SCRIPTURE: "So then, just as you received Christ Jesus as Lord, continue to live in him, rooted and built up in him, strengthened in the faith as you were taught, and overflowing with thankfulness." (Colossians 2:6-7)

OTHER SCRIPTURES: Colossians 2:7-15; 1 John 2:1-2; 1 John 3:1-3

WHAT JESUS MIGHT SAY TO YOU:

How did you come to me? Do you remember? You knew you needed me more than anything else you had in your life. You confessed your sins, and I forgave you for every one of them. I embraced you, adopted you, and made you part of my family.

So just like the day when you came to me—live like that with me today.

You still struggle with sin. I understand. It's reality. Confess it and bring it to me. I'm your defense lawyer. I speak to God, the Father, on your behalf. You are right with God only because of me. Watch yourself. Don't think that being busy with church activities makes things right with the Father.

You're NOT okay! But you *are* loved, accepted, and completely forgiven—and you need me every day. Not dealing with your sin every day puts static interference in our communication. It gets harder and harder for you to hear me. So confess your sins every day; keep that clear-channel reception with me.

Remember who you are. When you came to me, I gave you a radical new relationship with the God who created you. Don't let our relationship become "old news" in your life. I adopted you as my child. Everything I have belongs to you.

Get ready for the battles of life today. Focus on who you are now in this relationship with me. You don't have to earn my love and acceptance. You are a new creation, fully accepted, adopted into my family...and you are free. Trust me—it's true.

Your trustworthy Friend, Jesus

SUMMARY CHALLENGE: Don't let the problems of life scare you today—because you live under the protection and care of my heavenly Father.

JOURNALING OPPORTUNITY:

DEVOTIONAL 48

Praying 24/7

TOPIC: Praying without ceasing

MAIN SCRIPTURE: "Use every piece of God's armor to resist the enemy in the time of evil, so that after the battle you will still be standing firm. Stand your ground, putting on the sturdy belt of truth and the body armor of God's righteousness. For shoes, put on the peace that comes from the Good News, so that you will be fully prepared. In every battle you will need faith as your shield to stop the fiery arrows aimed at you by Satan. Put on salvation as your helmet, and take the sword of the Spirit, which is the word of God. Pray at all times and on every occasion in the power of the Holy Spirit. Stay alert and be persistent in your prayers for all Christians everywhere." (Ephesians 6:13-18, NLT)

OTHER SCRIPTURES: Luke 18:1-7; Romans 8:26-27; Galatians 4:6; Philippians 4:6-7; 1 Thessalonians 5:17; Jude 20

WHAT JESUS MIGHT SAY TO YOU:
Despite the intensity of a spiritual battle or how strong or weak you feel at any given moment, I have given you everything you need to live a godly life and to stand your ground against any attack from your Enemy, Satan.

With every piece of spiritual armor you put on, you clothe yourself with me. I am your helmet of salvation, your breastplate of righteousness, your belt of truth, your shoes of the good news of peace, your sword of the Spirit.

But wearing your spiritual armor still isn't enough. If you run into battle fully equipped but aren't in communication with your command center, you will lose. You need my guidance, my wisdom, my encouragement, and my strength. That's why it's important that you pray at all times and on every occasion in the power of the Holy Spirit.

Praying at all times means staying in constant communication with me: When you wake up, in between classes, during a test at school, while you're hanging out with your friends, when you go to bed. Prayer is more of an attitude than an activity. Satan loves to ambush my unsuspecting followers. Without prayer he will catch you off guard every time.

As you pray, avoid doing all the talking. I know you have a lot on your heart, but make room for the Holy Spirit to guide you in prayer. Spend time in silence so I can respond to you. But also remember that you're in the middle of a war, not just a fight. Other people face the same attacks as you. They need you to pray for them as much as you need them to pray for you.

But there's one more reason why we need to stay connected: I just like to spend time with you!

Your Source for everything, Jesus

SUMMARY CHALLENGE: Staying connected to Jesus is more of an attitude than an activity.

JOURNALING OPPORTUNITY:

DEVOTIONAL 49

Make Peace with Your Past

TOPIC: Feeling regret

MAIN SCRIPTURE: "God saved you by his special favor when you believed. And you can't take credit for this; it is a gift from God. Salvation is not a reward for the good things we have done, so none of us can boast about it. For we are God's masterpiece. He has created us anew in Christ Jesus, so that we can do the good things he planned for us long ago." (Ephesians 2:8-10, NLT)

OTHER SCRIPTURES: Psalm 103:10-14; Ezekiel 36:26-27; Acts 22:1-21; Romans 5:8; 2 Corinthians 1:3-4; 2 Corinthians 5:17; 1 John 1:7

WHAT JESUS MIGHT SAY TO YOU:
No matter how hard you try to hide it, ignore it, even fix it, you can't change your past. And I don't want you to because your past—your failures as well as your successes—makes you who you are.

Even when you thought you were all alone, I was with you... in your darkest hour...when you committed your most embarrassing sin...in the middle of your greatest humiliation.

I know the real you, and I died to free you from the chains of your past. You are now a new creation; the old has passed away and the new has come. Your past sins are completely wiped away from my memory.

But I will not erase your past from your memory because your scars can serve as reminders of my presence in your darkest hours. The memory of your most embarrassing sin tells you how much you need my forgiveness. The moments of your greatest humiliation remind you of the humiliation I endured to free you from your past and your sins of the present. And besides, how can you see how far I've brought you unless you have something to compare it to? Rather than grow bitter or embarrassed by your history, use it as an opportunity to grow closer to me. Use your experiences—both good and bad—to comfort others who are walking the same road you have walked.

Your Redeemer, Jesus

SUMMARY CHALLENGE: Embrace the present, don't hide from your past, and remember how far Jesus has brought you.

JOURNALING OPPORTUNITY:

DEVOTIONAL 50

Be the Friend You'd Want to Have

TOPIC: Needing a friend

MAIN SCRIPTURE: "How beloved and gracious were Saul and Jonathan! They were together in life and in death. They were swifter than eagles; they were stronger than lions." (2 Samuel 1:23, NLT)

OTHER SCRIPTURES: 1 Samuel 16:7; 1 Samuel 20:42; Proverbs 13:20; Proverbs 17:17; Ecclesiastes 4:9-12; John 15:12-15; Philippians 2:1-11

WHAT JESUS MIGHT SAY TO YOU:

I understand your desire for a friend. Here are a few thoughts to help you find one.

If you wait for a good friend to materialize suddenly before your eyes, you may have to wait forever. The best way to find a friend is to be one.

Look around you: Who do you already know that might need a friend? Don't judge people by their outward appearance—my Father in heaven sure doesn't. He looks at the heart. In the same way you may be surprised that people you assume would drive you nuts might actually grow on you once you get to know them.

The people who became my friends during my time on earth didn't fit the job description of the "proper" friends for the Son of God. They included tax collectors and fishermen—not exactly the most respected people back in my days on earth.

Let's look a little deeper into what kind of a friend you might want to be. Take a few moments and ask yourself, "What kind of a friend has Jesus been to me?" Hopefully words such as *loving*, *accepting*, and *forgiving* come to mind. Those qualities will serve you well in being—and finding—a friend. A good friend has the heart of a servant and is willing to sacrifice. Who wouldn't want a friend like that?

Don't get discouraged because you haven't found the right friend. Acquaintances are easy to find, but lasting friendships take time. In the meantime be the kind of friend to those around you that I am to you.

Your best Friend, Jesus

SUMMARY CHALLENGE: The best way to find a friend is to be the kind of friend that Jesus is to you.

JOURNALING OPPORTUNITY:

DEVOTIONAL 51

Too Soon to Quit

TOPIC: Needing encouragement

MAIN SCRIPTURE: "So when God desired to show more convincingly to the heirs of the promise the unchangeable character of his purpose, he guaranteed it with an oath, so that by two unchangeable things, in which it is impossible for God to lie, we who have fled for refuge might have strong encouragement to hold fast to the hope set before us." (Hebrews 6:17-18, ESV)

OTHER SCRIPTURES: Psalm 138:3, 7-8; Isaiah 43:2; Isaiah 51:12

WHAT JESUS MIGHT SAY TO YOU:

Living for me is like running a long race. Are you full of energy today or so tired you can hardly keep your legs moving? Life is more uphill than downhill. More headwind than tailwind. I lived here. I know how exhausting it can be.

But you're not running this race alone. Look for me standing beside the track. Do you see me? I'm cheering for you. It's too soon to quit. I'll give you extra strength to keep going and finish the race. I know you can do it with my help.

When you pray about your struggles every day, I hear your prayers and answer them. Read my Word and drink in my encouragement and strength. When you're surrounded by trouble or struggling with problems, I won't abandon you. I will be with you and bring you through. I made you. I won't let you be destroyed.

Don't be overwhelmed by any problem another person drops on you. You can handle it with my help. I calm your spirit and give you the confidence to face anything. Receive my encouragement and hold fast to hope until you see me face to face.

And don't keep all my encouragement to yourself! Spread some around. Build others up. Give love and care to the weak. Affirm those who doubt themselves. Be thankful in every situation. Cheer for your friends as I cheer for you. The more you give away, the more I will give to you. Your friends will ask where you get such a positive attitude and the grit to keep going. Tell them they can have it, too, if they come to me.

Cheering you on, Jesus

SUMMARY CHALLENGE: Be encouraged by God so you can give God's encouragement to others and build them up.

JOURNALING OPPORTUNITY:

DEVOTIONAL 52

Wiped Clean

TOPIC: Feeling shame for past mistakes

MAIN SCRIPTURE: "I am still not all I should be, but I am focusing all my energies on this one thing: Forgetting the past and looking forward to what lies ahead." (Philippians 3:13, NLT)

OTHER SCRIPTURES: Psalm 103:11-12; Romans 3:25; Romans 12:1-2; 2 Corinthians 5:17

WHAT JESUS MIGHT SAY TO YOU:

When you gave your life to me, I forgave everything in your past. Completely. Absolutely everything. All the dirt from your past, present, and future is washed away. Though your sins seem as scarlet they shall be as white as snow. My blood is a stain remover that wipes your life clean. Everything is forgiven.

In your shame your past defined who you were. Satan lied to you and personalized your sin. He accuses you and calls you a thief, a drunk, a hypocrite, whatever. If you believe that, you give him permission to keep you chained to your past.

In me you are a new creation. The old is gone. The new has come.

Your new life is defined by my righteousness. You are made good by me—by my blood. When I died, your sin was taken from you and poured into me. My righteousness (right standing with God) was poured into you. God has removed your sins as far away from you as the East is far from the West.

Your new life is not about your past. Your new focus is on the future, and your new life with me. You willingly presented yourself to me as a living sacrifice, so I can do with you whatever I want. And here's what I want—stop copying the behaviors and patterns of this world. Be a new and different person with a new freshness in all you do and think. Be like me. You will find out how satisfying this really is. It's what you were created to be.

Your Righteousness, Jesus

SUMMARY CHALLENGE: Your shame has been blown to oblivion. God does not see your past. Get your eyes focused on what God wants for you in the future.

JOURNALING OPPORTUNITY:

DEVOTIONAL 53

It Goes Beyond Love

TOPIC: Jesus doesn't just love you—he actually *likes* you!

MAIN SCRIPTURE: "The LORD your God is in your midst, a mighty one who will save; he will rejoice over you with gladness; he will quiet you by his love; he will exult over you with loud singing." (Zephaniah 3:17, ESV)

OTHER SCRIPTURES: John 15:13-16; Romans 8:31-39

WHAT JESUS MIGHT SAY TO YOU:
Let me ask you this: What do you think my reaction is when I hear your name? What is the expression on my face? Is it a look of disappointment? Am I rolling my eyes? Am I shaking my head? Am I thinking, "What a pain that one is!"?

How do I really feel about you? You may be thinking, "Obviously he loves me; it's his job to love me, but I would bet he's not very thrilled with me much of the time." You may be thinking this because you often feel that way about others. You probably love quite a few people in your own life because you feel like you should. But you don't necessarily like them all the time.

As hard as it may be to believe...I actually like you. It's true. When I hear your name, I get excited...so excited that my heart leaps, and I sing songs about you. Crazy, right? Well, it's true.

When I look at you, I feel blessed. Not only that, but there's nothing you could ever do to make me love you or like you any less. Nothing. No matter where you've been, no matter what you've done, no matter what you're going to do...my opinion of you will not change.

So the next time you imagine my reaction upon hearing your name...know that there's a giant smile on my face, a song on my lips, and joy in my heart. I like you...a lot!

Love, Jesus

SUMMARY CHALLENGE: Jesus thinks you're amazing; you can't do anything to change that!

JOURNALING OPPORTUNITY:

DEVOTIONAL 54

The Rumor of Jesus

TOPIC: Making Jesus contagious

MAIN SCRIPTURE: "He entered Jericho and was passing through. And there was a man named Zacchaeus. He was a chief tax collector and was rich. And he was seeking to see who Jesus was, but on account of the crowd he could not, because he was small of stature. So he ran on ahead and climbed up into a sycamore tree to see him, for he was about to pass that way. And when Jesus came to the place, he looked up and said to him, 'Zacchaeus, hurry and come down, for I must stay at your house today.' So he hurried and came down and received him joyfully. And when they saw it, they all grumbled, 'He has gone in to be the guest of a man who is a sinner.' And Zacchaeus stood and said to the Lord, 'Behold, Lord, the half of my goods I give to the poor. And if I have defrauded anyone of anything, I restore it fourfold.' And Jesus said to him, 'Today salvation has come to this house, since he also is a son of Abraham. For the Son of Man came to seek and to save the lost.'" (Luke 19:1-10, ESV)

OTHER SCRIPTURES: Matthew 5:15-16; John 13:35

WHAT JESUS MIGHT SAY TO YOU:
Who was Zacchaeus, and why was he so eager to see me? What had he heard about me? Who did he hear from? Why was he so intrigued by me?

He was a tax collector and considered a big-time sinner in his day, yet he was straining to see me. Why? He had never met me, but he had obviously heard of me. And whatever he heard was something so moving, so compelling, that he just had to see me for himself.

Zacchaeus must have heard about me from someone...or seen the evidence of me in someone's life. And it made him wonder. So I have a few questions for you: *Is the rumor of me so powerfully evident in your life that people long to meet me after spending time with you? Does your life make people want to climb trees and scale mountains just to get a glimpse of my face?*

When I was on earth, undesirables flocked to me. I was even called a "friend of sinners." These days sinners shy away from those who claim to follow me. Why is that? Are you doing something to counteract this?

Do you cause people to run to me, or are you like the disciples, grumbling and saying, "He has gone in to be the guest of a man who is a sinner" (Luke 19:7, ESV)? Does my love flow through you to others?

When you run to me as Zacchaeus did and understand your need for me, you'll be changed by my love, and my love will become evident in your life. When people spend time with you and experience this love, they will be attracted to my love as Zacchaeus was.

Live a life of contagious love! Pursuing you always, Jesus

SUMMARY CHALLENGE: Live a life of love so that others may join you in pursuit of me.

JOURNALING OPPORTUNITY:

DEVOTIONAL 55

True Satisfaction

TOPIC: Feeling jealousy

MAIN SCRIPTURE: "But if you are selfish and have bitter jealousy in your hearts, do not brag. Your bragging is a lie that hides the truth. That kind of 'wisdom' does not come from God but from the world. It is not spiritual; it is from the devil. Where jealousy and selfishness are, there will be confusion and every kind of evil." (James 3:14-16, NCV)

OTHER SCRIPTURES: Genesis 4:3-7; Proverbs 14:30; 1 Corinthians 13:4; Galatians 5:19-21; 1 Timothy 6:3-10; James 1:17; James 4:1-10

WHAT JESUS MIGHT SAY TO YOU:

I know it seems so harmless. No one has to know about it, and no one gets hurt when you exercise it (or so you think), so what makes it so wrong? What am I talking about?

Jealousy. Wanting something someone else has. It could be someone's good looks, intelligence, popularity, or girlfriend/boyfriend. It could be someone's clothes, car, or wealth. Whatever it is you desire, you know it's jealousy because it negatively affects the way you treat the person you're jealous of—usually with ridicule and resentment.

What makes jealousy so damaging? Do you think resenting someone doesn't hurt anyone? To be honest, it hurts you more than the person who makes you jealous. By burning with jealousy, you give the controls of your life to someone else. That person's presence drives you toward ridicule and resentment—

you just can't help yourself. And where jealousy lives, you make room for every kind of evil.

But your burning jealousy also tells me that what I have given you is not enough, that I am not enough. I am Lord of heaven and earth, and all of creation lies at my disposal! I love you so much that I give you exactly what you need. Just look at the cross—can't you tell that I have held back nothing from you?

Why do you aim so low, desiring only what exists in this life? What I want you to desire more than anything is me—not someone else's stuff, as if that could bring you the joy and contentment that only I can give.

So give up seeking what you know cannot satisfy and seek the one who does satisfy: Me.

Your contentment, Jesus

SUMMARY CHALLENGE: We can either desire someone else's stuff, which will never satisfy, or seek the only one who truly satisfies: Jesus.

JOURNALING OPPORTUNITY:

DEVOTIONAL 56

Whom Can I Count On?

TOPIC: Needing hope

MAIN SCRIPTURE: "Yes, dear friends, we are already God's children, and we can't even imagine what we will be like when Christ returns. But we do know that when he comes we will be like him, for we will see him as he really is." (1 John 3:2, NLT)

OTHER SCRIPTURES: Luke 18:35-43; Romans 5:2-5; 2 Corinthians 5:1-10; 1 Thessalonians 4:13-18

WHAT JESUS MIGHT SAY TO YOU:
Do you think I will keep my promises to you? (I don't want a quick, church-answer "yes.") Deep in your heart, do you believe I will keep my promises?

Broken promises are big. I understand why you hesitate to believe me. Some people you trusted have broken some big promises to you. Will I disappoint you, too? Good question. I don't mind you asking me.

The more you believe I will keep my promises, the more you have real hope.

Let's start with death. Are you scared? Does anyone really know what is going to happen? I'm the only reliable witness in the world who has been to both heaven and hell. You haven't seen either place. You only get one choice and one life to make that choice. When you listen to me and follow my instructions, you put your hope in me.

What about tomorrow? I give you free will to make choices tomorrow. If you listen to me and try to do what I say, it could be rough for you...loving people who aren't nice, saying no to getting high, forgiving people who hurt you, telling the truth, etc. Those are all right choices. Just one problem—doing what is right tomorrow might not make life comfortable. It might make life harder. Hope is believing me when I say that telling the truth and doing what's right will bring the best results in the future. That's hope. It doesn't run like a train schedule. Results show up eventually.

Want more hope? Read your Bible. It's my documented track record that proves my reliability. Start trusting me with big and small situations in your life. Pray. Obey. Wait. See what happens. You'll learn every day how much you can trust me.

Get ready. This will be the wildest adventure of your life.

Your Hope, Jesus

SUMMARY CHALLENGE: Hope is believing Jesus and his Word... every day.

JOURNALING OPPORTUNITY:

DEVOTIONAL 57

Rescue from Depression

TOPIC: Depression/feeling deep darkness

MAIN SCRIPTURE: "For you, O Lord, are my hope, my trust, O LORD, from my youth." (Psalm 71:5, ESV)

OTHER SCRIPTURES: Job 19:25-27; Psalm 23; Isaiah 60:1-2; Isaiah 61:1-3; Lamentations 3:21-24; Matthew 18:20; John 11:25; John 16:33; 1 Peter 1:3

WHAT JESUS MIGHT SAY TO YOU:

You feel as if you're swimming all alone in an ocean of darkness and despair. After treading water for so long, you're ready to give up and let depression's undertow drag you to unknown places, perhaps even death.

My friend, this is not the life I designed for you. You cannot free yourself from pain and hardship, but my desire is not that you spend your life drowning in an ocean of depression.

Please don't swim alone. You need to share how you feel with an adult you trust who can keep you afloat in the water, such as a parent, a teacher, or a youth pastor or volunteer.

It's also important to surround yourself with people who care about you. I know your depression tells you that no one cares, but I have placed people in your life who want to encourage you. To avoid assuming that they know what's going on inside, make sure you explain in detail how you feel.

Anytime two or three people gather in my name, I am present in a way that I am present nowhere else. That's why spending time with other people who follow me will help provide a net to pull you out of the water.

The night before I was nailed to the cross, I cried out to my Father and asked him if there was any way I could be delivered from the pain I was about to suffer. The stress was so great that I began sweating drops of blood.

The good news is this: I know your depression, and I carried it with me on the cross. You no longer have to carry it, so give it to me. I endured the cross so I could be your resurrection and life.

Believe my good news, Jesus

SUMMARY CHALLENGE: Jesus endured the cross so he can be your resurrection and life.

JOURNALING OPPORTUNITY:

DEVOTIONAL 58

Yes, You're a Failure— but You're in Good Company!

TOPIC: Failure and being a Christian

MAIN SCRIPTURE: "But he said to me, 'My grace is sufficient for you, for my power is made perfect in weakness.' Therefore I will boast all the more gladly about my weaknesses, so that Christ's power may rest on me. That is why, for Christ's sake, I delight in weaknesses, in insults, in hardships, in persecutions, in difficulties. For when I am weak, then I am strong." (2 Corinthians 12:9-10)

OTHER SCRIPTURES: Mark 14:43-46; John 21:15-19; Romans 3:23; Romans 8:1-11; Hebrews 12:1-2

WHAT JESUS MIGHT SAY TO YOU:

So you messed up again. Would it help to know that you're in good company? In my greatest hour of need all of my disciples either betrayed me or abandoned me. In fact, every person who sought to follow my Father in heaven has messed up badly: Moses, Abraham, Sarah, David, Mary Magdalene, Paul.

I say this not so you'll take sin lightly; sin is serious, and your sin cost me my life. But how can I reject you? You're family! You belong to me because I purchased you with my blood on the cross. So stop beating yourself up and questioning whether I've rejected you.

But here's what I want you to do: Admit that you can't live up to my standards. I would rather you know how messed up you are than for you to be messed up and not realize it.

Look to me for strength. My power is made perfect in weakness. As long as you try to will yourself into obeying me, you won't be able to do it.

Let me live through you. You can't live a godly life, but I can, and I've made my home in the deepest place of your heart. Abide with me, yield yourself to me, and make me the focus of your life. And don't focus on your sin.

Brush yourself off and get back in the race. Don't give up just because you stumbled. Life is not a sprint, it's a marathon— so get up and keep on running!

Your failures will only make you stronger if you choose to respond to them correctly. But don't ever forget: You will never wear out my willingness to forgive you.

Your strength, Jesus

SUMMARY CHALLENGE: You can't live a godly life on your own, but Jesus can—and he wants to live his life through you.

JOURNALING OPPORTUNITY:

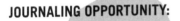

DEVOTIONAL 59

Safe Sex

TOPIC: Setting proper sexual boundaries

MAIN SCRIPTURE: "Daughters of Jerusalem, I charge you: Do not arouse or awaken love until it so desires." (Song of Solomon 8:4)

OTHER SCRIPTURES: Psalm 119:9; John 10:10; 1 Corinthians 6:18-20; Ephesians 5:1-20; Hebrews 13:4

WHAT JESUS MIGHT SAY TO YOU:

I see the sexual messages society repeatedly tries to pound into your head. Society wants you to think that sex is simply a physical act, that there's nothing wrong with premarital sex. Don't believe it.

I'll get straight to the point: Premarital sex is sin. I'm not trying to make life miserable for you, but your heart isn't ready to handle the intimacy of a sexual relationship. Awakening your heart before the time is right will have devastating effects—including in your life with the person you eventually marry. Trust me.

So let's construct some boundaries together before you pass the point of no return:

1. *Invite me into your relationships.* I didn't come so you would have an unsatisfying life; I came so you might have an abundant life. And besides, I'm present in all your relationships—don't you think it's about time you acknowledge me in them? Make me an active part in your conversation, and you'll discover a spiritual dimension of your relationship that few couples enjoy.

2. *Don't ask how far you can go.* When you do that, you're looking for ways to get around me. Instead stay far enough from the boundary that you won't have to ask that question. (Of course, asking me for a little insight doesn't hurt.)

3. *Take time to get to know the other person.* Usually when a premarital relationship becomes sexual, the two people stop exploring each other's hearts.

4. *Do things in groups.* This will go a long way toward preventing you from placing yourself in compromising positions.

5. *Ask your friends to help you stay pure.* They're an important line of defense.

You have a lifetime of enjoyable sex ahead of you. Don't put it in jeopardy by prematurely exploring it. And remember: If you've already explored, I love you just the same as I always have—just ask for my forgiveness and start your life and relationships anew.

Love, Jesus

SUMMARY CHALLENGE: Jesus wants you to enjoy a lifetime of sex—but he doesn't want you to lessen the joy by having sex before you're married.

JOURNALING OPPORTUNITY:

DEVOTIONAL 60

How Can I Know That Heaven and Hell Are Real?

TOPIC: Questioning the existence of heaven and hell

MAIN SCRIPTURE: "The acts of the sinful nature are obvious: sexual immorality, impurity and debauchery; idolatry and witchcraft; hatred, discord, jealousy, fits of rage, selfish ambition, dissensions, factions and envy; drunkenness, orgies, and the like. I warn you, as I did before, that those who live like this will not inherit the kingdom of God. But the fruit of the Spirit is love, joy, peace, patience, kindness, goodness, faithfulness, gentleness and self-control. Against such things there is no law. Those who belong to Christ Jesus have crucified the sinful nature with its passions and desires." (Galatians 5:19-24)

OTHER SCRIPTURES: Matthew 7:13-14; Mark 9:43-48; 2 Corinthians 5:6-10; 1 Thessalonians 1:5-10; Hebrews 11:13-16; James 1:17

WHAT JESUS MIGHT SAY TO YOU:

It's so easy to assume that this life is all there is. Believing in something or someone you cannot see or touch or smell requires faith. But heaven and hell are real places, and their existence affects your daily life.

Every time someone cuts you down...every time you stretch the truth or tell a lie...every time you prefer yourself to others... every time you do what you know is wrong...you prove the existence of hell. You see, hell isn't just a faraway place that "bad" people go to. Hell and Satan are the source of all evil in the world. And deep inside, your sinful nature craves this place—but it will only destroy your heart and drive you away from me.

Every time you encourage someone...every time you tell the truth, even when it hurts...every time you prefer others to yourself...every time you do what you know is right...you prove the existence of heaven. Heaven isn't a faraway place, either. Everything good and right and beautiful comes from my Father in heaven. Deep inside your redeemed spirit craves this place, and as you draw closer to me, you will recognize other glimpses of heaven in your life.

The existence of good and evil in this world proves that heaven and hell exist because they must come from somewhere—or someone.

Your Way, your Truth, and your Life, Jesus

SUMMARY CHALLENGE: So walk by faith, not by sight. This world isn't even your home; heaven is. So live that way.

JOURNALING OPPORTUNITY:

CONCLUSION

What Is 3Story®?

The heart of the matter: no rules, no formulas, just relationships

At its heart 3Story is a way of living life. It's a framework for understanding the process of change we experience in our relationships with God and with other people. Out of a relationship with Christ and relationships with other people, an amazing, heroic Christian life happens naturally: one life touching another life, "life-on-life ministry."

Think of three circles representing three stories:

God's story, my story, and their stories. The more the three circles overlap, the more a person can experience and see the power of the gospel of Jesus Christ.

- 3Story begins with a rich understanding of the content of three stories, with crucial focus on the most important story of all—God's story.

- 3Story connects people and stories—me and my story to God and God's story, me and my story to my friends and their stories, my friends and their stories to God and God's story. The more these stories and lives connect, the more powerful the impact of the gospel can be.

- The way we share the gospel is as much a sign of the good news as what we say.

- 3Story is not new; it is a return to a way of living that characterized Jesus' life and the lives of his disciples.

3Story is a different way of understanding life as a follower of Christ. Rick Richardson in his book, *Evangelism Outside the Box*, summarizes the bottom line for living a 3Story life: "We must first be good news before we can preach good news."

The three circles represent the content, the stories, of three lives. Within these three stories something will be revealed or we'll learn something about three people and three relationships. We can learn to make important relational connections that will enable us to live 3Story lives.

At the end of the story—
3Story is first and always about abiding in Christ, taking our life breath from him, living our lives through him, and loving and listening to him first, always with the help of his Holy Spirit.

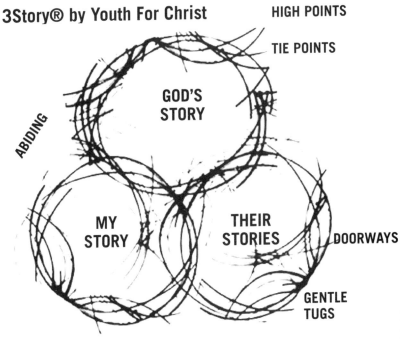

3Story® by Youth For Christ

HIGH POINTS

TIE POINTS

GOD'S STORY

ABIDING

MY STORY

THEIR STORIES

DOORWAYS

GENTLE TUGS

DISCOVER THEIR STORIES THROUGH LOVING AND LISTENING.

DISCLOSE MY STORY BY BEING REAL AND TALKING ABOUT JESUS.

10 shifts in faith-sharing that emerge from 3Story
based on 2 Corinthians 5:14-21

1. It's stories more than steps. Acts 17:27-28
   3Story is about bringing three stories together in a natural way. It is not about taking people through a sequence of predetermined steps.

2. It's honesty more than perfection. Philippians 3:9, 12-13
   3Story asks the believer to be honest, not perfect.

3. It's them more than you. 1 Thessalonians 2:7-11
   3Story allows our friends to be who they are as we discover their stories.

4. It's questions more than answers. John 4:1-30
   3Story is more about asking questions than giving answers. Christians often offer answers to questions that not-yet-followers of Christ aren't even asking.

5. It's listening more than telling. Colossians 4:6
   3Story starts out with listening, not preaching. It's built on the assumption that people listen to people who listen.

6. It's hope more than judgment. 1 Peter 3:15-16
   3Story is primarily about my sharing my need for Jesus and my hope in him rather than my judging others' lifestyles, words, or choices.

7. It's the Holy Spirit more than program. Romans 8:26-30
   3Story means being led by God's Spirit in our relationships. We don't work through tips or techniques to maneuver God into a conversation. 3Story is about bringing Jesus' story into a relationship at just the right moment.

8. It's circular more than linear. John 4:1-30
   3Story invites people to discover parts of Jesus' story that are most relevant to them at that moment. Jesus' story doesn't come to everybody in the same order or with the same words.

9. It's love more than knowledge. 1 Corinthians 13
   Not only in a postmodern world but also from a biblical worldview, love wins people's hearts.

10. It's contributing more than controlling. 1 Peter 3:15-16
    3Story is not about controlling, rather it's about allowing conversations to be free enough to flow and naturally bringing Jesus into those topics or discussions.

INDEX

Where Do I Find It?

CONVERSATIONS WITH JESUS

THE MINISTRY OF YOUTH FOR CHRIST

With a passion to reach every young person, one at a time, Youth for Christ/USA® www.yfc.org has been operating local ministry centers across the country since 1944. Today's most widely practiced programs include Campus Life®, City Life®, Teen Parents® and Youth Guidance®. YFC/USA is also one of over 100 fully-charted nations, participating in the international movement of Youth for Christ, providing opportunities to serve around the world through Project Serve® www.projectserve.org and World Outreach www.yfcworldoutreach.org. For more information about 3Story® visit www.3story.org.

CITY LIFE®
YFC's City Life helps young people in urban communities through teaching life skills, building relationships with caring adult role models, providing opportunities for positive peer group experiences, and sharing the Good News of the Gospel of Jesus Christ.

TEEN PARENTS®
YFC's Teen Parents connects trained adults with pregnant girls and teenage parents in programs designed to help them make good choices and establish a solid foundation in Christ, not only in their lives, but also in the lives of their babies.

YOUTH GUIDANCE®
YFC's Youth Guidance reaches troubled young people through juvenile justice and social service agency contacts. Youth Guidance connects them with trained adults who help them make good choices and find healing and new life in Christ.

YFC's PROGRAMS

INCLUDE:

CAMPUS LIFE®

YFC's Campus Life combines healthy relationships with creative programs to help middle school and senior high young people make good choices, establish a solid foundation for life, and positively impact their schools for Christ. Campus Life is a place to make friends, talk about everyday life and discover the beginning of a life-long relationship with Jesus Christ.

YFCAMP® [yfc.org/camp]

YFC's YFCAMP is a new national initiative that exists to create an outdoor environment that invites God to transform the lives of young people through shared experiences, outdoor challenges, and times of solitude. Additionally, local YFC ministry centers host numerous camps around the nation.

WORLD OUTREACH [yfc.org/worldoutreach]

YFC/USA's World Outreach serves YFC International, sending missionaries to serve as an integral part of indigenous YFC ministries in nations spanning the globe from Bolivia to New Zealand.

PROJECT SERVE® [yfc.org/projectserve]

For three decades, YFC's Project Serve has sent thousands of young people and adults on mission trips in partnership with over 90 indigenous YFC ministries.

MYM AND MCYM [yfc.org/mym]

YFC's Military Youth Ministry equips ministry centers in the USA with resources and training to reach military youth in their community. And, in partnership with Military Community Youth Ministries, MYM places youth workers on military bases around the world.

LOSER'S CLUB IS A REAL-LIFE LOOK AT BIBLE CHARACTERS
SUCH AS MOSES, SOLOMON, DAVID, THOMAS, RAHAB, AND
OTHERS. EACH VIGNETTE REVEALS PEOPLE WHO STRUGGLE
WITH WEAK FAITH, CONFUSION, AND FRUSTRATION. THESE
STORIES WILL HELP STUDENTS CONNECT WITH THESE
FLAWED HEROES, FIND ENCOURAGEMENT IN THEIR
STORIES, AND GET INSPIRED BY GOD'S LOVE AND CARE FOR
"LOSERS."

The Losers Club
Lessons from the Least Likely Heroes of the Bible
Jeff Kinley

RETAIL $9.99
ISBN 0-310-26262-3

Visit www.invertbooks.com or your local bookstore.

INTRODUCING THE ONLY NIV BIBLE SPECIFICALLY FOR TEEN GIRLS AGES 13-16. TRUE IMAGES COMBATS THE WORLD'S FALSE IMAGES BY POINTING GIRLS TO GOD'S MESSAGES ABOUT WHO THEY ARE, WHERE THEY ARE GOING, AND WHAT THEY ARE WORTH IN HIS EYES. THESE TRUE MESSAGES BRING LIFE, HOPE AND HAPPINESS BY HELPING THEM STRENGTHEN THEIR RELATIONSHIPS WITH GOD, FAMILY, FRIENDS, AND GUYS.

TRUE IMAGES HAS LOADS OF SPECIAL FEATURES AND AN INFORMATIVE WEB SITE WITH ADDITIONAL RESOURCES ON MANY OF THE FEATURE TOPICS, BIBLE READING PLANS, LINKS TO OTHER SITES AND MORE!

True Images SC
The NIV Bible for Teen Girls
Livingstone Corporation, General Editor

RETAIL $22.99
ISBN 0-310-92816-8

Visit **www.invertbooks.com** or your local bookstore.

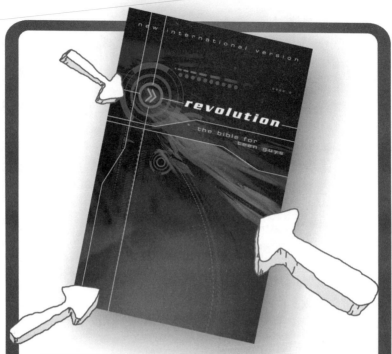

INTRODUCING THE ONLY NIV BIBLE SPECIFICALLY FOR TEEN GUYS AGES 13-16. REVOLUTION REVEALS GOD AS THE ULTIMATE REVOLUTIONARY AND PROVIDES A ROAD MAP FOR EVERY GUY TO LIVE A REVOLUTIONARY, HARD-HITTING, DIFFERENCE-MAKING LIFE BY READING HIS BIBLE. THIS BIBLE INCLUDES SPECIAL FEATURES THAT ADDRESS RELEVANT ISSUES FACING GUYS TODAY: FRIENDS THAT GET THEM INTO TROUBLE, ENEMIES WHO MAKE LIFE MISERABLE FOR THEM, RULES THAT SEEM TO SPOIL THEIR FUN, PARENTS WHO DON'T UNDERSTAND, AND MORE.

REVOLUTION HAS LOADS OF SPECIAL FEATURES AND AN INFORMATIVE WEB SITE WITH ADDITIONAL RESOURCES ON MANY OF THE FEATURE TOPICS, BIBLE READING PLANS, LINKS TO OTHER SITES AND MORE!

Revolution SC
The NIV Bible for Teen Guys
Livingstone Corporation, General Editor

RETAIL $22.99
ISBN 0-310-92820-6

invert

Visit **www.invertbooks.com** or your local bookstore.

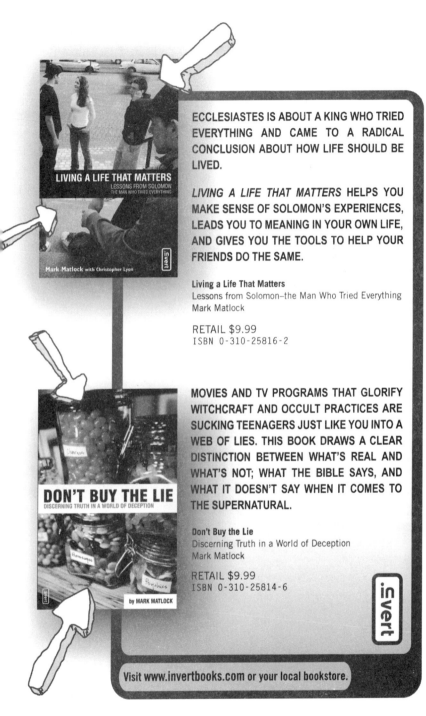

ECCLESIASTES IS ABOUT A KING WHO TRIED EVERYTHING AND CAME TO A RADICAL CONCLUSION ABOUT HOW LIFE SHOULD BE LIVED.

LIVING A LIFE THAT MATTERS HELPS YOU MAKE SENSE OF SOLOMON'S EXPERIENCES, LEADS YOU TO MEANING IN YOUR OWN LIFE, AND GIVES YOU THE TOOLS TO HELP YOUR FRIENDS DO THE SAME.

Living a Life That Matters
Lessons from Solomon—the Man Who Tried Everything
Mark Matlock

RETAIL $9.99
ISBN 0-310-25816-2

MOVIES AND TV PROGRAMS THAT GLORIFY WITCHCRAFT AND OCCULT PRACTICES ARE SUCKING TEENAGERS JUST LIKE YOU INTO A WEB OF LIES. THIS BOOK DRAWS A CLEAR DISTINCTION BETWEEN WHAT'S REAL AND WHAT'S NOT; WHAT THE BIBLE SAYS, AND WHAT IT DOESN'T SAY WHEN IT COMES TO THE SUPERNATURAL.

Don't Buy the Lie
Discerning Truth in a World of Deception
Mark Matlock

RETAIL $9.99
ISBN 0-310-25814-6

invert

Visit www.invertbooks.com or your local bookstore.

IT'S NOT THAT YOU DON'T WANT TO READ THE BIBLE, MAYBE YOU JUST DON'T KNOW THERE'S MORE THAN ONE WAY TO READ IT.

ENJOY THE SILENCE

A 30 DAY EXPERIMENT IN LISTENING TO GOD

MAGGIE ROBBINS
DUFFY ROBBINS

ENJOY THE SILENCE'S 30 GUIDED EXERCISES PLUG YOU INTO THE ANCIENT DISCIPLINE OF LECTIO DIVINA. EACH LESSON PROVIDES A SELECTION OF SCRIPTURE, PROMPTS FOR MEDITATION, A CHANCE TO LISTEN TO GOD, AND A WAY TO RESPOND TO WHAT YOU'VE READ.

Enjoy the Silence
A 30 Day Experiment in Listening to God

Maggie Robbins, Duffy Robbins

RETAIL $9.99
ISBN 0-310-25991-6

Visit www.invertbooks.com or your local Christian bookstore.

SECRET POWER TO JOY IS ABOUT FINDING THE JOY ONLY GOD CAN GIVE. YOU'LL STUDY THE BOOK OF PHILIPPIANS AND LEARN GREAT STUFF ABOUT HOW THE HOLY SPIRIT HELPS BELIEVERS FIND REAL HAPPINESS DESPITE WHAT'S GOING ON IN THEIR LIVES OR ON THEIR HEADS.

Secret Power to Joy, Becoming a Star, and Great Hair Days
A Personal Bible Study on the Book of Philippians
Susie Shellenberger

RETAIL $9.99
ISBN 0-310-25678-X

THIS BOOK WILL HELP YOU FIGURE OUT WHAT DOES AND DOESN'T FIT WITH BEING A CHRISTIAN. YOU CAN DO THIS STUDY AT YOUR OWN PACE BY YOURSELF, WITH A FRIEND, OR WITH A BUNCH OF FRIENDS.

Secret Power to Treasures, Purity and a Good Complexion
A Personal Bible Study on the Book of Colossians
Susie Shellenberger

RETAIL $9.99
ISBN 0-310-25679-8

AUTHOR SUSIE SHELLENBERGER LEADS GIRL READERS, AGES 13 TO 17, ON AN ENGAGING EXPLORATION OF 1 PETER. THROUGH HER TRUE-TO-LIFE ANECDOTES AND FUN ASSIGNMENTS, STUDENTS WILL COME TO REALIZE THAT HAPPINESS AND SUCCESS COME BY DRESSING THEMSELVES WITH THE CHAMPIONSHIP ATTIRE THAT THEIRS BECAUSE OF WHAT JESUS DID ON THE CROSS.

Secret Power to Winning, Happiness, and a Cool Wardrobe
A Personal Bible Study on the Book of 1 Peter
Susie Shellenberger

RETAIL $9.99
ISBN 0-310-25680-1

invert

Visit www.invertbooks.com or your local bookstore.

Book 1: 'Nama Beach High
New Girl in Town

Nancy Rue

RETAIL $6.99
ISBN 0-310-24399-8

Book 2: 'Nama Beach High
False Friends and True Strangers

Nancy Rue

RETAIL $6.99
ISBN 0-310-25180-X

Book 3: 'Nama Beach High
Fault Lines

Nancy Rue

RETAIL $6.99
ISBN 0-310-25182-6

Book 4: 'Nama Beach High
Totally Unfair

Nancy Rue

RETAIL $6.99
ISBN 0-310-25183-4

A SERIES OF FICTION FOR TEENAGE GIRLS, THE
'NAMA BEACH HIGH BOOKS ARE ENGAGING AND
ENTERTAINING. BOOKS 1-4 FOLLOW THE LIFE OF
LAURA DUFFY AS SHE MOVES TO A NEW SCHOOL AND
GETS A NEW JOB AND A SECRET ADMIRER. FOLLOW
DUFFY ON HER ADVENTURES AS SHE MEETS NEW
FRIENDS, AS WELL AS GOD, AND LEARNS WHAT IT'S
LIKE TO ADJUST TO A NEW PLACE AND A NEW FAITH.

Visit www.invertbooks.com or your local Christian bookstore.